OSWALD EARLY

The Messenger

The World War 1 diary of a wireless operator

Compiled and edited by Russell Early

MEREO

Cirencester

Mereo Books

1A The Wool Market Dyer Street Cirencester Gloucestershire GL7 2PR
An imprint of Memoirs Publishing www.mereobooks.com

The Messenger: 978-1-86151-235-2

First published in Great Britain in 2014
by Mereo Books, an imprint of Memoirs Publishing

The address for Memoirs Publishing Group Limited can be found at
www.memoirspublishing.com

The Memoirs Publishing Group Ltd Reg. No. 7834348

The Memoirs Publishing Group supports both The Forest Stewardship Council® (FSC®) and
the PEFC® leading international forest-certification organisations. Our books carrying both the
FSC label and the PEFC® and are printed on FSC®-certified paper. FSC® is the only
forest-certification scheme supported by the leading environmental organisations including
Greenpeace. Our paper procurement policy can be found at
www.memoirspublishing.com/environment

Typeset in 11/16pt Bembo
by Wiltshire Associates Publisher Services Ltd. Printed and bound in Great Britain by
Printondemand-Worldwide, Peterborough PE2 6XD

Oswald S. Early, my grandfather, served with the 1/9th Battalion Territorial Force of the Royal Hampshire Regiment as a Wireless Operator during the First World War. On February 4 1916 the Battalion sailed from Devonport, Plymouth, for India, where it was engaged on the North West Frontier. My grandfather spent the rest of the war serving in India, Iraq and Afghanistan, finally returning to the UK to be demobbed in October 1919.

Throughout his adventures my grandfather kept a diary, which gives us a vivid picture of life in the Battalion, the trials, the tedium, the hardships and occasional horrors of the campaign in India and on the Eastern Front and the challenges and dangers he faced.

Russell Early

FOREWORD

This diary has been copied from my original diaries which I kept during my service abroad. It contains an account of my life in the British Army from November 1914 to October 1919.

In memory of the boys I knew.

We are the dead, short days ago
We lived, felt dawn, saw sunset glow
Loved and were loved, and now we lie
In Flanders Fields.

Take up our quarrel with the foe,
To you from falling hands, we throw
The torch; be yours to hold it high
I ye break faith with us who die
We shall not sleep, though poppies grow
In Flanders fields.

- From 'In Flanders Fields', by Lt Col John McCrae

Oswald S. Early

GETTING READY FOR THE OFF

NOVEMBER 16TH 1914

I joined the 3/9th Hampshire regiment at Bournemouth and was sent to Southampton, where I was kitted out etc and billeted at the Nelson's Arms for nearly 2 weeks. Then I went to Chichester where the regiment was stationed and stayed in Adelaide Road with a Mrs Cobden. I stayed in Chichester until the beginning of January 1914 and then I went to Arundel to start a course in Musketry. We stayed here about a week. I passed out 2nd in the shooting test of our draft.

I was then posted to E company of the 1st Battalion and moved to Bognor, where we were engaged in coastal defence duties. Being a cyclist Battalion we trained for this work. I found E company at the Princess Mary's Home at Bognor, they had stations at Pagham, Felpham etc. We had to patrol at night from Pagham to Selsey, Bognor to Felpham. At Felpham there was a lookout on the beach, and this looked out onto Littlehampton, where we met patrols of another regiment.

I went out to Felpham for a month or so on detached duty. From here I went back to Bognor and then to Chichester again, as the Battalion were concentrating there. I was billeted in South Street, near the museum. While here we used to go to Goodwood Park every day for drill, practising attacks etc.

I spotted a submarine while I was on the coast between Bognor, had to get on the phone to Portsmouth to give a description of it. We had a fairly decent time about here and the fellows in the Battalion were a very decent lot.

We left Chichester about the beginning of April 1915 for Brighton, where our company stayed in an empty house in Salisbury road. Here we had to patrol the coast to Shoreham Bridge one way and to Black Rock and Newham Bridge in the other direction. We also had a guard on the Palace pier and a patrol along the front at nights.

I didn't care a lot for Brighton, but I suppose being in the army makes a lot of difference. We stayed here a few weeks and then the Battalion moved on to Hastings. We were billeted at the Highland Mansions, St Leonards. These houses were fine old-fashioned places built of stone. They were of course empty.

Some of our fellows are at Eastbourne and at various places along the coast. We had to patrol the coast from Newhaven to Rye Harbour. We had stations at Seaford, Cuckmere, Beachy Head, Eastbourne, Cooden, Hastings and Pett. We had to cycle out very often to Battle Abbey. There are some very large caves near Hastings and a guide will take you round for 1/-. They are very interesting.

Fairlight is rather a pretty place. It is near the sea and there are some nice walks there under the trees. We had a shooting range near there. From St Leonards I went out to Pett, where I stayed about 3 weeks. We lived in tents here near the coastguard station. After this I went back to Hastings and then to Bexhill, where we stayed in a large empty house on the sea front. We stayed here for 3 weeks and then went out to Cooden for a week. This place is about 2 miles along the coast from Bexhill. From here we went back to Hastings and after two weeks we went down to Alfriston, which is an inland village about 4 miles from Seaford.

We stayed at Solly Joel's empty racing stables, and whilst here we used to cycle into Seaford every day, to dig trenches along the cliff, beach etc. We have dug trenches all along the south coast from Selsey Bill to Rye. We did not have any beds with us at Alfriston, so we had to sleep on straw.

From here we again returned to Hastings and after a month or two we went to Seaford, where we stayed in a house on the front. We used to do a patrol to Newhaven from here. Seaford was a very quiet place and there was nothing to do at night. There were a lot of black troops stationed near here. They came I believe from East Indian and they had a quite a good opinion of themselves, swanking about the streets with walking sticks etc.

From there we went out to Cuckmere Haven, where Lord Kitchener's private cable entered the sea to France. From here I went to Beachy Head near the coastguard's station and then to Eastbourne, finally getting back again to Hastings. I had a very nice time during my stay in Hastings, quite the best during my stay in England, and we seemed to get on very well with the people there.

We stayed at St Leonard's until November 1915, when we had a chance to go on Surries if we went as infantry. We all volunteered to go as infantry, so we handed our cycles over to another regiment and moved off to Chiseldon on the Marlborough Downs. We had a good send-off from Hastings. When we arrived at Chiseldon we found it knee-deep in mud in places. We lived in wooden huts here, but they were very comfortable. We did three months of hard training here, haring long route marches around Avebury and Marlborough and Swindon. Once we had orders to proceed to France, but we were recalled after we had marched some miles. I managed to get home for Christmas on overseas leave as we were bound for the east.

CHAPTER TWO

SETTING SAIL
FOR INDIA

1916

Feb 1st - Left Chiseldon with full marching orders with 16th Hants band in attendance at 3 am. We were eight in a carriage, which combined with our equipment made it rather cramped. We arrived at Exeter early in the morning and stayed for tea and cakes etc, which were provided by the Mayoress. We arrived at Plymouth 10.30am and went on board the SS Ceramic, a White Star liner of 18,000 tonnes. We stayed here the night.

Feb 4th – We can see the men and cadets at drill in the naval barracks from the deck.

4 pm - left the quay. Tugs towed us to the harbour mouth. From here we proceed under our own steam.

6 pm - Getting out into the Channel there are 2 destroyers with us. The training ships in Plymouth gave us a good send-

off but our fellows did not cheer much. If we had been going to France we should have been in much better spirits. Can see Eddystone Lighthouse now.

Feb 5th – Out of sight of land going SW. I had a fairly decent night but did not feel too bright in the morning.

8.45am – On guard (submarine) for 24 hours. We are in the Bay of Biscay now and the ship is rolling and dipping badly.

11 am – Seasick for the first time in my life, and it isn't a very pleasant feeling.

Feb 6th – Feeling all right this morning. Came off guard, a lot of fellows are ill today. They are lying about the deck. We are steering a very erratic course just lately.

Feb 7th, 8:45 am – On guard (lookout). Passed two ships, but they were too far away to see what they were. Haven't seen anything of our escort ship Devonport. Our people evidently rely on the speed of the ship, which I understand can steam 22 knots.

6 pm – Curtains put up all around the ship to prevent any lights being shown to prevent our ship being recognised by anyone on shore, as we are now getting near Gibraltar.

Feb 8th – Passed Gibraltar at 4 am. We passed close to Curta on the African coast and had a good view of it and the hills about it. A small French patrol boat came out from Gibraltar to see who we were.

2:30 pm – Inoculation for cholera.

Feb 9th - 7:45am – On guard. The weather is colder today, passed close to French convict island not far from the African coast. All smoking on deck stopped after 5:30 pm. Steering a zig zag course, land has been in view several times during the day.

8pm– Boat stations alarm, I was having a bath at the time and had to make a dash for a life belt and get on deck with about half my clothes on, the captain of the boat said we turned out very smartly, we are supposed to wear lifebelts always,

Feb 10th – On guard. Weather fine but cold.

5pm– Approaching island with a lighthouse on its western side. We are now about 100 miles SW of Malta. Letters are being collected to be censored prior to them being put ashore at Malta.

Feb 11th – On guard midnight to 4 am, saw lights off Malta before coming off guard.

7 am – We are at Valetta now and am putting ashore a fellow who has gone mad, also our mail. We have a nice view of the town. Can see St Paul's Church? Hospital ship Panama in harbour near us.

10 am – Raining rather hard, going N.E.

4pm– Going S.E., there was a heavy storm during the night.

Feb 12th – 7 am – going S.E. Weather cloudy, orders out that everyone is to go about without boots or socks.

Feb 13th – Going S.E. Weather fine. Letters in for going ashore tomorrow and Port Said.

10:30 am – church parade, but no singing allowed.

9pm– Getting cloudy. On guard till midnight.

11pm– Going very fast. I understand that a submarine is after us, it will have to move to catch us. We have our machine guns on the saloon decks.

Feb 14th – 3:30 am – arrived at Port Said. 8 am – In harbour. There are a lot of ships here. A battalion of troops is embarking near us for the Persian Gulf. Left off wearing lifebelts for the first time and guards have now stopped. Heard we were chased by a sub last night but nothing happened. Dismantled the naval gun which we had in the stern and sent it ashore.

A lot of natives in boats are all around our boat trying to sell us sweets, fruit, cigarettes etc. They throw a rope which is fastened to a basket up on the deck and we put money in the basket and let it down to them. The natives puts in whatever one wants and the fellow on the ship pulls the basket up again.

A few are going ashore. The streets of Port Said are absolutely filthy – it is the dirtiest place I've ever seen. The people are filthy in looks and habits.

3:30pm – Large boat bound for London passed us with passengers and troops and they gave us a good cheer. Concert on deck this evening and lights are allowed for the first time. We hear that a troopship has been torpedoed between Gibraltar and Malta.

Feb 15th, 7am – Left Port Said. We are in the canal now and have to go very slow, the canal is about 80 yards wide so there is not room for two ships of this size to pass.

10am – Passed entrenchments and troops. We called up the troops by FLA and found they were the East Yorks, West Yorks, Worcester Yeomanry and Durham Light Infantry that gave us a good cheer. There is a railway running close to the canal on the Egyptian side and one running across the desert on the Arabian side, evidently made by the troops.

2pm – Passed a large camp of Australians, who gave us a splendid reception and had their band playing on the bank. They played "Australia" and "Auld Lang Syne" and we threw them a lot of cigs, some of which fell into the canal, but the fellows swam after them. There are a lot of Indians about on the banks. Saw a mountain in the distance (Sinai?)

6:30pm – Arrived at the salt lake. There are a lot of smaller boats here.

7pm – Anchored for the night, portholes kept open for air as it is getting warm. Starting to wear helmets. Concert by our own Battalion this evening. We have on board besides our own Battalion the 1/25 Londons and the 2/6th Sussex cyclists.

Feb 16th, 7:30am – moved off past a battleship and a troopship. There is a big range of hills on the Arabian side, and the country on the other side is very flat for some miles and then it rises into what appears to be a plateau or ridge of hills. In the canal again, big camp of English troops on both sides, London Yeomanry and London sharpshooters.

2pm – Suez in sight. Passed three warships, Glory, Jupiter, and Minerva.

2:30pm– Stopped at Suez and put ashore goods and took Capt. Campbell on board. There was a boxing contest during the afternoon on board and a concert by the Londons and Hants in the evening. I hear that the Ceramic is the largest boat that has ever been through the canal. The length of the canal is about 100 miles and the cost of taking a boat through is 8/- per ton. Saw a big suction dredger which is used to flood the desert when an enemy appears.

17th Feb – passed lighthouse at entrance to Gulf of Suez.

6:15am – Medical inspection parade in shirts and helmets only. It is getting hot now.

2:30pm Parade in full marching order, heat enough to make one swoon.

6:30pm – Concert by the Sussex, putting draught shields out of portholes, going to sleep on deck tonight, too hot below.

Feb 18th – 4:30am – Nearly got drowned by the men who wash the decks. They use a big hose pipe and give one about 3 seconds to get up and pack up one's bed.

1:30pm Inoculated again, saw a lot of flying fish and dolphins.

Feb 19th – Very hot. Hope to reach Aden tonight.

10am – passed a lot of islands called the Twelve Apostles, saw a shark swimming near the boat.

3pm – Passed islands known as the Devil's Gates.

8pm – Lights ahead, believe it to be Persia. There is a lighthouse which flashes 4 times and then pauses for about 6 seconds, they signalled for permission to ask who we were.

Feb 20th – Passed Aden last night, we are now in the Indian Ocean. We can still see land to the north. Band played for the first time. The sea is beautiful and as calm as a pond.

Feb 21st – Not quite so hot today. Going E now.

Feb 22nd – weather very nice and sea beautiful. Boxing competition.

Feb 23rd – gave in letters for posting at Bombay.

Feb 24th 11:30am – land in sight, also fishing boats.

4pm – anchored in Bombay Harbour. We have a good view of the town

Feb 25th – 6am- On fatigue at Hatchway.

7am – Moving in towards the docks.

8am – going through a lock gate which has to let us through. An Indian sold us papers - he tied them to a stone and threw them on board.

10:30am – Parade with Battalions for marches through

Bombay for exercise. The streets in some places are very dirty, we only saw two white people. Some of the buildings are fine in the principal streets, especially in the Victoria railway station.

3pm – Changed our money into Indian money at the YMCA rooms at Alexandria Bocks, bananas are 6d, vests 4 for 1/-.

8pm - Parade in full marching gear, I had a telephone and flags to carry. We marched for nearly a mile to the train, which we entered about 9:15pm. The carriages are very long with seats running from end to end. Carriage holds 24 men with kits but I do not see how we can all sleep at one time, there is not enough room. We are bound for Bangalore, a place about 650 miles away in south India.

10pm – Trying to get some sleep, some fellows are on the floor under the seat.

12pm – stopped at Poona. Cannot get to sleep, it is scandalous travelling like this.

Feb 26th – 7am – Reached Dhond and had some tea, the scenery is very wild. Passed some banana and coconut trees.

11am – Ponialvadi

2pm – Sholpur

2:30pm – Hotei

6pm – Gulbarga

Later we reached Wadi, where we had bully beef and bread and tea. We have only had a piece of bread and jam for the last 24 hours. We are not allowed to buy anything from the natives such as fruit etc.

10pm – too hot to sleep, so we put our heads out of the window to get air.

Feb 27th – 6:30am, passed Kupal. There are ranges of rocky hills on both sides, the country is more cultivated here.

7pm – Passed Adoni, Apsari, Guntakal, June

Feb 28th – Reached Bangalore after going nearly into Madras. We have come the longest route.

9am – Helping to unload our signalling gear, and afterwards went up to the barracks as guard to it. All our kit etc. was taken along in bullock carts. The heat on the way from the station was horrific, and to make things worse we were dressed in dirty clothes.

2:30pm – dinner, the best I've had in a long time. One has to be very careful when carrying any food about in the open as there are hundreds of hawks about and they will swoop down and take it out of one's hand or off the plate.

Feb 29th – Parade in full marching order for march, some fellows went down before we started. The dust was very bad and getting into one's throat etc.

3pm – Medical inspection.

March 1st – Parade for signalling, recd. Rs22 pay, wrote letters. Not allowed to leave barracks owing to measles.

March 2nd – 6:45 am – Signalling.

11am – Lecture by MO on India.

1pm – Measured for drill suit by native tailors.

5pm – dog and stick walk for about 6 miles.

March 3rd – As usual wrote letters. Went out in the evening for a long walk with Sid H – saw a shooting which looked like a rocket.

March 4th – 6:30 am church parade. The food isn't very good now and we have to buy to make up.

March 5th – As usual there are thousands of flies here.

March 6th – Practice with field telephones and Exchange. Companies go for a march to Bangalore city.

March 7th – 6:30 – signalling, Battalion at drill, played cricket in the evening.

March 8th – Barrack inspection by the Colonel, joined RATA. There are two more measles cases in our bungalow.

March 9th – 6:30 am – played cricket for our platoon against no. 3. We lost by 30 runs.

7:30pm - Pictures at RATA.

March 10th – As usual – went to Rajah zoo in the afternoon.

5pm – Played hockey for A company.

March 11th – Signalling. 5pm – played hockey in Battalion match, officers vs men. We won 6-3. The evenings are beautiful here.

March 13th – The Bishop of Madras conducted our church service yesterday. He spoke very well.

March 14th – Bought some stuff at bazaar today, went for a walk in the evening.

March 15th – Wrote letters. Lecture in the evening by the Bishop of Madras on the Indian religion.

March 17th – St Patrick's Day. Had a stroll to one of the Indian villages near here. They are filthy. The women run away from us, but the men look at us as savage as they can, as if they would like to hit us over the head, but I have a revolver and always carry a stick.

March 18th – as usual. Signalling etc.

March 19th – There are two picture houses in Bangalore.

6:30pm - dinner service. Joined the tennis club.

March 20th – Went to Bangalore and bought silk scarf, saw a native procession.

March 22nd – 6:15 am – parade for GOC inspection and march past.

March 23rd – Usual parades, went into bazaar in the evening and bought some silk etc.

5pm - played hockey against St Joseph's College, won 2-1

March 25th - Issues out with Glengarry caps, sent parcel and letter home.

March 27th – Holiday owing to Colonel's birthday.

March 29th – Played hockey for signals vs. No.1 and No.2 Platoons - we won 8-1.

March 30th – Holiday – Had a stroll around the village near here. It is in a filthy state. The people have no idea of sanitation or cleanliness and live crowded in little mud huts into which the cattle, fowls etc. Go when they like. I shouldn't think the natives ever wash themselves and it is impossible for them to buy soap.

April 4th – 8:15 – Paraded with Battalion and marched to the Mardan to take part in the Proclamation Parade in honour of the landing of the new Viceroy.

8:45pm – Invited to officers' quarters for the evening, get back at midnight.

April 8th – There was a heavy thunderstorm in the night and it is raining now.

April 10th – Heard that the S.S. Simba has been sunk with the mail.

April 13th - Played hockey for signals.

April 14th – Sidney Grosse left for Wellington as signal instructor.

April 15th – No letter yet. I suppose they have gone down, Hyde of B company died and buried today.

April 16th – 6:15am – Church parade. 9:10am - Teddy Graske shot himself through the head. I heard the rifle go off and rushed into his room to see what was up and found him on the floor with the rifle under him. He had put the muzzle of the rifle into his mouth and blew the top of his head off. He had been on the drink for some time and couldn't pull himself up. He was one of the best, as long as he kept off the drink.

5pm – Paraded as one of the firing party for the funeral. All A Company attended. The Colonel made a speech at the grave. Sgt Jupe Roberts and Burridge gone on signalling course at Wellington.

April 18th – went down to Ulsoos to see native festival and procession of the big carts. It was very interesting to see the carts that the priests ride. They are huge with very large wooden wheels. They arc pulled through the streets by the people, who throw fruit, food, coins, etc. up into them.

The road is lined with diseased people and beggars who call out for money etc. they make an awful noise. Years ago babies used to be thrown under the wheels of the carts to please the gods, but the brutes have stopped this practice. Crowds of gaily (and otherwise) dressed natives follow the carts, singing and shouting and some of these fellows work themselves into such a state sometimes that they go practically mad.

May 2nd – Signal section inspection by the Brigadier (Col Crocker). 3pm – Heard General Townsend has surrendered.

May 18th – My birthday. Hope to be home on my next.

May 19th – Instructing A company signalling.

May 21st - received letters

May 22nd – Route march.

May 24th – Empire day – 11am – Caught a snake 4ft long on Agram plain.

5pm – Played hockey against no.2, received letters

June 1st – Out on communication work between D company and the barracks. There are nine of us here in a small hut.

June 2nd – Getting used to our letters home now. It is rather nice here, we have to cook our own food etc. and then watch it to see that the monkeys or birds don't go off with it. Going to another place tomorrow.

June 3rd, 7pm – Arrived at our new camp, and put the tent up. We are in a little wood which is swarming with monkeys. An old woman came along just before dark and told one of our fellows who understood Tamil that there was a devil living in the wood and it would kill us if we stayed there the night. He told her the devil would catch it if he came along whilst we were there.

June 4th – Have run a telephone line to C company camp five miles away. We are in touch with the barracks at

Bangalore by helio and lamp. Had the latest war news through on the Lamp tonight.

June 5th – raining hard. I think we go back to barracks tonight.

June 6th - Marched out about 8 miles with Battalion and Devon battery RFA. We bivouacked for the night and kept in communication with artillery by lamp.

June 7th – Turned out at 4am and started an attack which finished about 9am. We then marched back to barracks. A few fellows went down through fatigue when we arrived. Wrote letters.

9:30pm - heard news that Kitchener and his staff had been drowned.

June 12th–16th - Out on a scheme keeping communication between A company and barracks. We have made a little hut out of sticks, grass etc. But it is rather draughty. I shall try and get a small tent out from Bangalore.

June 17th – Arrived back in barracks and had a good sleep, the first I've had for a long time

June 20th – Going out on another scheme. On communication work between B company and Bangalore. When we were looking for a nice place to fix up our own station I trod on a small cobra, but I didn't give it much time to bite me - I soon cleared off to a safer place.

June 22nd – Back in barracks we were inspected by the inspector of army signals today (Col Grant) and read letters, papers etc.

June 24th – Out on a scheme about 8 miles away, we left barracks at 5:30 am and returned at 3pm. We didn't have anything to eat all the time.

June 26th – Lecture by Miss Grighton cheerfully about babies, I don't know what the idea was to talk to us about it.

June 28th – Heavy rain last night.

5pm - Played hockey.

June 29th – Out on scheme with Battalion bivouac for the night.

June 30th – Marched all day and did an attack , bivouac for the night.

July 1st – Marched nearly all day and got back to barracks about fed up. Received letters.

July 5th – Read letters. hear that Chas Bradley has got the DCM. I often wished I had joined the Yeomanry and gone out with them.

July 6th – sent letters and photos home. Sussex regiment left here on 160 mile journey by road to Mysore city and back. Our football team left for Calcutta to play for the shield.

July 10th - wrote letters. The food we are getting now isn't fit for a dog. We have to buy a lot.

July 11th – concert in RATA rooms.

July 12th – route march from 8:30am to 2:30pm.

July 13th – Read letters.

July 15th – Our football team drew against 1/5th Hants at Calcutta.

July 19th – Have got rather a bad knee after falling when playing hockey.

23rd-24th July - Battalion out on Divisional scheme.

26th July - Battalion out on a scheme we arrived back at night about done here have been on the move all day.

July 29th – Our football team lost at Calcutta in the semi-final.

August 1st – Minden Day. Wore roses in our helmets today, sports were held on the polo ground.

August 4th – second anniversary of the war, services were held in most of the churches here.

August 5th – a lot of fellows have gone sick lately, owing I believe to a change in the weather.

August 6th-10th – weather very dull.

August 11th and 12th – Going to my course at Agram. Missed my marksman badge by 3 points.

August 16th – Draft arrived from England. They are looking as brown as we are.

August 19th – Inoculation at the hospital this morning. My arm is getting stiff and I am not feeling too bright.

August 20th – Feeling better this morning but arm very stiff.

August 23rd – On range with telephones. We turn the lines from the firing point into targets.

August 25th – Beat Indians at football 2-0.

August 26th – Our football team drew with the Sussex in the final of the Brigade tournament.

August 28th – We lost the replay with the Sussex 1-0. This is the first time our team has been beaten by anyone in the Brigade. After the match the Sussex marched past our barracks with their band, they are the worst lot of sportsmen I've seen.

August 29th – Just heard that Rumania is coming in with us. They ought to help things along in the Balkans.

August 30th – Inoculated for typhoid. Mails arrived from Bombay today, a lot of the Sussex are down with paratyphoid here. Owing to a dispute about our large number of marksmen as compared with other regiments in the Brigade, our platoon is to fire in a competition with the same numbered platoon in the Sussex, Kents and Londons.

August 31st – our no 12 platoon on the range today made a bigger score than the rest of the Brigade put together, so they know who are the best shots now.

Sept 5th – I was getting some butter today from the dairy and when I came out I was putting some change in my purse when a hawk swooped down and took the butter and purse out of my hand and flew off with them. Next day someone returned my purse, which they had found about ½ mile from where I lost it.

Sept 15th – The plague is about in the city and also in a village near here. We have to give notice if we see any rats or fleas. One of our camp followers died with plague today.

Sept 16th – The plague is spreading. The exits to barracks are patrolled to keep all natives out.

Sept 17th – Went to communion at Trinity Church.

Sept 20th – Battalion route march. Got wet through three times but one's clothes dry out in about ½ an hour.

Sept 27th – Bought sandalwood boxes etc. at the bazaar. When buying anything out here one must be prepared to argue about the price for an hour or so, as the natives always tells you the price of an article is at least 6 times its value and one has to beat him down to a reasonable figure. I myself have beat a native shopkeeper down from R24 to R5 for a table cloth. Some of the high class Indian shops will sell their goods at fixed prices.

Oct 3rd – Battalion route march. We went 25 miles and it was rather warm work.

Oct 6th – 6am - Packing up kits etc. to move to Hebbal, a place two miles away. We go under canvas there.

11am – at Hebbal, pitched tents.

Oct 7th – It rained in torrents during the night and many tents were washed down. I woke up to see my kit and various other articles floating about, the water being a foot deep in the tent. We have now dug trenches around the tent.

Oct 14th – Sunday signalling practice, as we are going in for a test in a few days.

Oct 17th – Out with the Battalion all night on a scheme.

Oct 18th – 4pm – Went down to Harris barracks Bangalore for signalling test.

7pm – At Harris barracks. We are to stay here for about three days and we have to sleep in a school room where lectures are held. It will be all right, there are no scorpions about, but they have a liking to get into one's bed when it is on the floor. Best to look into one's boots before putting them on as they very often get into them.

Oct 19th – Had large flag sending test and small flag sending test.

10am – Small flag reading test with telescope.

11am – semaphore reading test.

Oct 20th – Buzzer reading test – 10 words per minute.

Dummy test – 12 words per minute.

9am - semaphore sending

10am - Helio setting up and aligning

7:30pm – Lamp reading test

Oct 21st – 9am – Station work test.

10am – Cable laying test.

11am – Map reading test. This is the finish, we go back this evening. The food here is a lot better than we have been used to in the Battalion.

5:30pm – Arrived back in camp, wrote letters.

Oct 26th – Received letters from England.

Oct 28th – we played no 12 platoon in the hockey tournament, drew 1-1 after a hard game. The war news has not improved much just lately.

Oct 29th – Church parade. Our padre cannot preach a decent sermon to save his life, he is so dry that no one takes any notice of him. When we were at Bangalore we used to go to St Marks church on Sunday evenings and some of the white people wrote to the vicar to say that they objected to us flooding the church. The vicar replied in church and said he would rather preach to us than he would the civilians, and told them if they didn't like it there were other churches to which they could go.

The civilian population, chiefly English, treated us very bad when we arrived in the country. We were not allowed inside any library or club and the white women seemed to think we were animals or something worse - they would never speak to any of us. Lately however, having found out what class of fellows our regiment contained, they treated us rather better and invited several fellows to the bowling social club to play tennis etc. and we were allowed into the library.

Nov 1st – A draft arrived from England to join us, our band met them at the station.

Nov 2nd – P.D. and myself won the 1st and 2nd round of the shooting competition, but my partner let us down in the final round. Lecture by the Bishop of Madras on England during war. He has just arrived from England. Our Battalion shooting team beat the Kents, Londons, Sussex, Oxford and Bucks, Bangalore rifles and the Kalar Goldfields.

Nov 3rd – Received letters. Saw a leper go along the road here, his flesh was sort of whitish pink.

Nov 11th – Raining in torrents today.

Nov 13th – Parade for Battalion photo as the last one proved a failure. There is a rumour about that we are going to the north of India soon or to Europe. I hope it will be Europe. Bombay (Hainsworth), Ken Level, Parsons and Lush left for Poona to join the R.E. signals.

Nov 16th – wrote letters. Proficiency pay starts today.

Nov 17th – read mail.

Nov 19th – Went to communion. Very cold today.

Oct 24th – Cycled out to Hundi Drooge, a mountain about 30 miles from here, with Stevens, Sell, Farrah. We left our cycles at the bottom and got an Indian to guide us to the top, which we reached about 5:30pm. It was getting dark and we were about done. There is a dark bungalow up here, but the native did not have any food, so we got him to send down to village for some.

6:30pm – a native came to tell us that one of our fellows was about halfway up the hill and couldn't get any further. We knew who it was - it was Howe, who had told us he would be coming on later. We managed to procure a lantern and we went down to find him. When we reached him he was about done and was going to stay whcre he was for the night. We however got him to the top, where the native had got some hot coffee ready so we all drank about a quart each and then waited for some curry and rice, which seemed delicious. Later on we turned in, in a sort of vault which was very damp, but we borrowed three mattresses each, one under and two over, so we slept fairly warm.

Nov 25th – 7:30am – Chota Hazrei (Breakfast) of curry, rice and cakes. We are in the clouds here this morning one cannot see for more than a couple of yards.

11am – Mist clearing.

12:30pm – Got into communication with camp by helio, camp is 32 miles away.

3:30pm Tiffin (Lunch). There is a splendid view from here.

The height of this place is 6000ft and now the weather is clear and one can see for many miles. Hundi drooge is an old stronghold of a former King named Lippu Sultan and it was captured by the British in their conquest of southern India. There is a very thick wall all around the top of the mountain. This wall is loopholed for the defenders to use. The inside is comprised of vario0ur temples etc. and in the centre is a very large open air bath with steps leading down all the way around. This bath is about 50 yards square and was evidently used by Lippu and his household. Another interesting place is a narrow ledge where Lippu used to take his prisoners and if they wouldn't join him and twin Mohammedans he would throw them over. There is a sheer drop of several hundred feet to the rocks below. It is understood that thousands have been thrown over here.

Oranges, melons etc. grow on the hills here. The Dak bungalow built and owned by Mrs Cutton of Bangalore is partly finished, I believe he used to live up here during the hot weather. Had a good dinner consisting of chicken and rice. Going back to camp now.

9pm – Back in camp. We had to ride in the dark most of the way as we had no lamps.

Nov 26th – farewell speech by Gen Phayre, so we are evidently going to move at last.

Nov 27th – I am going to run for my platoon in the Battalion team race tomorrow. Ran 3 miles for practice. There is a little wood near here in which there are thousands of flying foxes – the trees are black with them.

Nov 28th – 4:30pm – Started on the run, which consisted of a paper trail, lost nearly half a mile owing to false trail but managed to finish first out of our team. The distance was about 6 miles.

Nov 30th – Mother's birthday, hope she is having a good time. The Londons, Sussex and Kents are going up country with us.

Dec 1st – Packed up as we are going up country tomorrow, went to Bangalore to see the picture 'Battle of the Somme'.

Dec 2nd – Left Hebbal for train station, several civilians came to see us off, it was rather different to our reception. We are rather sorry in a way to leave here as this place is considered one of the best for troops in India. The climate is rather decent - the temperatures seldom rises over 100 degrees in the shade. The country around is very tropical, coconuts, bananas, oranges, mango and sea is largely cultivated. Birds such as parrots and parakeets abound, have also scorpions, snakes, centipedes etc. On the journey now we have passed Malur, Tyakul, Boweringpet and Jelapet. We had a meal at the latter place. We are now running between two mountain ranges. Passed Mailpatti and Katpadi.

6:30pm - Dark now and train is shaking badly.

7:45pm - reached Arkonam near Madras. it is very hot here and there are no fans as we are travelling in 2nd class Indian carriages.

Dec 3rd – passed a large a lake and iron bridge.

8:30am – Vanqunaa

8:50am – Tadpatri

10am – Rayalcher Uyu, stopped here for breakfast.

11:20am – Gooty

1:20pm – Guntakal June, at a place called Tungabhadra, a native bought fruit and gave it to us. Some European fellows gave us some Embassy cigarettes. Passed river Kistna. Stopped for dinner at Raichur and later stopped at Wadi. There are no cushions of any sort in these carriages and the seats are composed of plain wood.

Dec 4th – Passed Hotei, Sholapur, Kurduwadi, stayed at Dhond for tea and bread and cheese.

4:15pm – Armednaqar. Small camp of English troops here.

Dec 5th – Khandwa – stayed for breakfast. It is very cold this morning and frost is on the windows.

11:30am Harda

2pm – Itarsi – stopped for tea and to pick up rations. We cross the Vindlya mountains here, crossed the Nerbudda river.

4:30pm – Barkhera – rather cold here as it is on top of the mountains. We had three engines to pull our trains up. There are a lot of old peacocks here.

6:30pm Bhopal – Stopped for tea. As we were going through the station one of our fellows who had an egg served to him for tea threw it at a native who was dressed up and waiting for a train. It hit him and made rather a mess, while we all laughed.

Dec 6th – Gwalior – we stayed here an hour or so, I saw Aja Man Singh Palace and the fort on the hill. I bought some native coins here - as this is a native state they used their own coins.

11am – Agra – we are going to have a look round Agra. As we have a few hours to waste the colonel is taking us round.

7pm- Just got back from our tour. We visited the Taj Mahal and the fort and came back through the town. The Taj is a wonderful building of white marble and it took 20,000 men 20 years to build it. The height of the dome is 250ft and there are four towers, each 164ft. There is a marble pathway about 36ft wide with fountains which lead up to the Taj from each of its entrance gates, which are also huge affairs. The Taj was built by the Mogul emperor Shah Jehan as the burial place of his wife and himself. Mumtaz Mahal was the name of his wife, and means jewel of the palaces. It was designed by a Persian. The fort is very interesting. The pearl mosque is here and is considered to be very fine work, it is also made of solid white marble. The emperor Shah Jehan was imprisoned here by his son, and from his room he could see the Taj where his wife was. There are a few British soldiers in the fort on garrison duty.

8:10pm – Left for Delhi. Train is jolting badly.

Dec 7th – 1am – Delhi. Stayed for about an hour, stopped at Amballa for breakfast. We saw the conspirators of the Lahore case and they tried to spit at us. It is very cold at nights now.

2:45pm – Jullunder – passed big banana plantation. I have a bad headache and cold, shall be glad when the journey is over.

6:20pm – Lahore. Stayed for tea for an hour or so.

Dec 8th – passed the Chenab river

6:30am Rawalpindi – the country is beginning to look bare, and there are hills on each side.

9:30am – Burhan – This is our destination and it looks a rather wild spot.

6pm – The dust here is awful, being nearly 2ft thick, and it fills the air and nearly chokes one. We are to sleep 12 men to a tent with our rifles tied to us to prevent the natives stealing them. Our railway journey was 2300 miles.

7pm – turned in as we have no lights. We have four blankets each as it is so cold.

Dec 9th – Turned out to have our rifles checked and put under a guard. It is like an English winter's day ice being on the water this morning. Received letters.

Dec 10th – Church parade. The colonel told us we should be here for about three months. We had a fairly decent place to bathe, a snow stream called the Haro river, and the sun during the day makes it fairly warm.

Dec 11th – Wrote letters. A Battalion of the Gurkhas joined us today. They frequent the hills around the camp. This is a very wild place with practically no vegetation except close to the road. The people about are chiefly Pathans and live in caves out in the hills and in mud huts etc. There is a very large village about a mile from the camp and also several smaller ones in the district. The women are dressed in Mahommedan style, wearing trousers and veils.

Dec 12th – made a fireplace outside our tent.

Dec 13th – Battalion making roads through the camp.

Dec 14th – received parcel from home.

Dec 15th – orders out that everyone is to carry 5 rounds of ammunition always.

Dec 16th – Inspection by Sir. J. Munro, CIC of India.

7pm – raining hard.

Dec 17th – The ground is hard today owing to the rain. The CIC spoke to us on church parade. He said we were a smart Brigade but too young to go on with the Surries yet. He said we must not keep asking to go on Surries as we were doing our own duty where we were and that people in England knew they could rely on us to do our own bit. This looks like staying in India for some time.

Dec 18th – out on a scheme before the staff Battalion orders today says that companies must take ammunition on schemes in case of attacks by outlaws.

Dec 20th – Battalion granted leave for ten days. Wrote letters, got leave to visit Delhi.

Dec 21st–23rd – there are snowbound mountains to the north east of us and when the sun rises they are tinted a beautiful pink colour.

Dec 24th – 200 geese are killed for Xmas dinner. Some of our fellows went to Pindi yesterday and some of the cafés wouldn't sell them anything because they were common soldiers. In one café some of the Indians were having tea when some English women came in, but they wouldn't have their tea in the same place as soldiers, so they asked an officer to turn the fellows out. These are the sort of women we have come 7000 miles to defend. I should like the natives to rise and liven some of these people up. They would soon come to us for protection.

Dec 25th Xmas day – I wonder where my next one will be. We had a decent dinner consisting of goose, ham and vegetables followed by duckling.

6:30pm – lit up a big bonfire and held a sing song around it
.

Dec 30th – our company held a practice fell de joye as they are leaving on Monday, which is the anniversary of the raising of the Indian army.

CHAPTER THREE

1917

Jan 1st – 8:30am – paraded with company and marched to Divisional parade. The Division tried a fell de joye followed by artillery salute.

Jan 3rd - out all day on a scheme.

Jan 6th - Londons gave a concert at the YMCA.

Jan 7th - Brigade church parade, the dust is a foot high.

Jan 8th - went out ten miles on a scheme over rough ground. We had to wade through the River Haro.

Jan 9th - out on a scheme. We did 30 miles over hills and dongas and we were about fed up by the time we arrived in camp.

Jan 10th - concert by the London Regiment.

Jan 12th – scheme for hill fighting. Did about 24 miles and waded in the river twice.

Jan 13th – our concert party gave a show at the YMCA. 200 camels arrived today.

Jan 14th — received parcel from home. We can see snow on the mountains – they look beautiful some mornings.

Jan 17th - annual signalling test. We did most of the reading and sending today.

Jan 18th — finished test, sent parcel home.

Jan 19th — result of test was 18 first class, 6 second class, but we don't know yet who are the firsts and seconds.

4pm — had a test on telephony as the Colonel didn't want so many firsts, so he got the signal officer to give us an extra test. We hope to hear results in a few days.

Jan 20th — Wilts battery arrived to join us.

Jan 21st — raining. Bloomfield, Knibbs, Bartlett and Clark gone to Divisional Signal Company.

Jan 23rd — out on a scheme against the Londons.

Jan 25th — cable scheme to Burham village. Mail in.

Jan 27th — results of signalling test:

FIRST CLASS. (A company) A Knibbs

A Early
B Hodges
C Wyatt
C Bartlett
D Bowman
D Hartlett

SECOND CLASS A Farrah

B Bloomfield
B Birch
B Stevens
D Carter
D Clark
D Harding

The remaining ten failed through telephony.

Jan 29th – Scheme to Famra village. Bivouac for the night. Had to keep communication with Brigade headquarters day and night. From our position we could see the River Indus quite plainly.

Jan 30th – Didn't sleep much last night as we had to turn out owing to alarm and it was very cold. Out on scheme all day and bivouacked again for the night.

Jan 31st – couldn't sleep last night, too cold. Going back to camp this evening.

4pm – back in camp. Read letters.

Feb 2nd – inspection by the Chief of the Indian staff.

Feb 5th - went out towards Pindi to make a Brigade camp.

Feb 6th – out on a big scheme today, marched 10 miles and bivouacked, was on guard with lamp during the night.

Feb 7th – food sent up for the picquet, but none for us as the cook had packed up when we went down, but the adjutant got me some food at the officers' mess. Battalion got back to camp at 6pm. We have been marching all day and have done well over 30 miles. It was one of the hardest days we have done.

Feb 12th - Brigade scheme.

Feb 14th - Big Brigade scheme, 8am to 6pm. We got back absolutely fed up as we had to climb a hill which was over 1000ft and as steep as a roof.

Feb 15th – Bombardier Hainsworth died at Bombay.

Feb 16th – all day Brigade scheme, started out at 10am and got back 11pm.

Feb 18th – the 2/1st Gurkha bagpipes band played this morning. They are very smart and many of them had been to France.

Feb 19th – scheme from 9am to 7pm, finished fed up as usual.

Feb 21st – scheme 9am to 5:30pm.

Feb 22nd – paraded just before midnight for scheme. We went across country for about 12 miles and attacked a hill 1000ft high at dawn.

Feb 23rd – arrived back at camp at 10:30am.

Feb 25th - scheme with the 6th Hants battery, met L Munetern.

Feb 26th – Battalion scheme. I have had about enough of these stunts - I suppose they think we never get tired. D company beat C company Kents in the semi-final of the YMCA cup 5-0. I won a sweep on the match.

Feb 27th – Night stunt with the Gurkhas, who are very decent little fellows. They think a lot of Englishmen and will always help one with Indians. They are good fighters, three times as good as the average Indian.

Feb 28th – Sid H gone to Cambellpur to join the machine gun corps with about half our machine gun section.

March 1st – medical inspection, as we are going on Divisional operations on Saturday, wrote letters.

March 2nd left Battalion with Brigade (45 Infantry) for a place called Hassan Abdul on the Pindi road.

4pm - in our new camp. We are in 160lb tents, 16 men per tent, so we are packed like herrings at night.

March 4th – couldn't get to sleep last night as it was so cold. 7pm, heard there is trouble on the frontier – I hope we go there.

March 5th - paraded for scheme but was recalled to camp. Had to pull down our tents and stand by. I hear we are off to the frontier. The Sussex are leaving. We shall have to bivouac tonight.

March 6th – awaiting orders. The Sussex left by train for the frontier, also the Gurkhas.

2pm – orders out to return to Burham immediately.

7pm – back at Burham.

March 7th – standing by 10am, tents are off to the frontier. Had orders to pull down our tents and pack up. Later on we had orders to put them up again, so I suppose we are not wanted now.

March 9th – parade as usual, the flies are getting rather saucy now and it is getting hot.

March 12th – Paraded in full marching orders and 100 rounds of ammunition, marched about 15 miles and did an attack for a mile Then marched back to camp over 7 miles of dongas. I am rather tired this evening. This was Kitchener's test.

March 13th – Too tired to sleep last night - sounds strange but it is a fact.

March 14th – very hot today. We have to wear helmets in the tents during the day.

March 15th – we had a terrific dust storm today which covered everything and our clothes, blankets etc. are full of it. Left for Peshawar. We went to the soldiers' home and got permission from the political agent to go up the Khyber pass tomorrow. Had a look round the city - it is a very wild place and it is not safe for fellows to go there unless it is in the day and there is a party.

March 16th, 8:30am – left for the pass in tum tums rind of trap and two ponies. The road is a fairly decent one to Jamrud

Fort, which is at the entrance to the pass. A few miles out of Peshawar is a large college for Indian students. On our arrival at Jamreid fort we had to show our passes and sign our names in a book. We had a look over the fort - it is in communication with Peshawar church by helio and CC lamp. Jamrud is 10 miles from Peshawar.

Just past this fort we enter the pass, which consists of two roads (the motor road and the caravan road) running between the mountains. There are a lot of caves here in which the Pathans live. All the natives one sees here are armed in some way. Some have Winchester repeaters, there are shotguns etc. and we saw one of them had a bow, in the string of which he had a small pouch which he used to shoot stones. I asked him to show me how he used it, but he couldn't shoot very straight. The Khyber rifles guard the pass on Tuesdays and Fridays, these days the caravans come through from Kabul and Peshawar.

Arrived at Ali Musjid, a fort another 11 miles past Jamrud. I saw the Afghan caravan come through here and also one going back to Afghanistan. They chiefly use the Afghan camel to carry the goods, a smaller and more stoutly-built camel than the Indian or Egyptian camel. Ali Musjid is the farthest point anyone is allowed to go unless on military duty. There is another fort at the other end of the pass called Landi Kotal. Arrived back in Peshawar 5:30pm and we hired a gharry (Pony trap) and visited the gardens, zoo etc.

March 17th – 7am breakfast, had a stroll around before going to the station. We travelled back in the dining car and had dinner there. We had a splendid view altock and River Indus and we also saw the River Kabul at Howshera. Arrived Burham in afternoon.

March 18th – we are on the move again, this time I believe to the Simla hills. The dust storms here are awful and one cannot see across the tent - they continue for hours. Jim Stevens, Aby and Birch Hartlett gone to Prona with the REs.

March 19th – dust storms all day, going tomorrow.

March 20th - Packed up 3:30pm and B and D companies moved off by train. At 8:30pm we moved off after enduring a dust storm all afternoon. We are going to Dagshai, a place about 400 miles from here.

March 21st – 8:20 am arrived at Jellum, we stayed at Lahore 2½ hours and had a stroll around. Crossed the Jellum and Chenab rivers between here and Pindi.

Amritsar - stayed here for tea. Stopped at Jullunder, met Bert Newman here, Passed Amballa. We are going to Dagshai, a place in the Simla Hills.

March 22nd - reached Kalka at the foot of the hills. We got out here and stayed all day and put up small tents. Staying here tonight and marching to Dagshai tomorrow. A light railway runs up to the mountains for here to Simla.

March 23rd – Moved off for Dagshai, which is 20 miles up the hills. Arrived in the afternoon. It has been a rather tiring march, being uphill all the way with the last three miles like the roof of a house. It is 6000ft up here and the view of the plains is beautiful.

March 24th - wrote letters. There was a fall of snow on a hill here last night.

March 25th - church parade. It has rained hard nearly all day and it is very cold. We can see Kasauli from here, also Solon and Sabathee. Two of our companies are staying here while the other two are going on to Jutoh near Simla.

March 26th - Raining hard.

March 28th - Had a look around the place, there is a soldiers' home and a Roman Catholic institute here where one can buy supper etc and also a bazaar, but it is a very small one. The hills about here are covered with a kind of pine tree and various fruits grow wild such as pears, plums and a kind of raspberry. There are practically no white people here owing no doubt to it being winter.

March 30th wrote letters, weather beautiful today.

April 1st-8th - usual parades.

April 9th - had a heavy thunderstorm during the night and the lightning was very vivid.

April 10th - inspection of station by A.D.A.M.S.

April 12th - played billiards against the sergeants tonight for the details team. Lost my game by four points.

April 14th – got into communication with Kasauli by helio.

April 16th – Played billiards against our second team, won my game by 22 points.

April 18th – raining hard today

April 19th – there was a terrific lightning storm this evening, the sight was wonderful.

April 21st – played billiards against no. 112 platoon, won my game by 30 points.

April 22nd to May 10th – Parades as usual – nothing special happened.

May 11th – there was an earthquake shock here at 2am this morning, which made the earth shake,

May 13th – I hear that a village was destroyed in the Punjab by the earthquake the other night.

May 14th – Our tennis court opened today.

May 15th – We act as transmitting signal station Kasaule and Solon now. We keep up communication all day.

May 20th – played billiards against 12 platoon. I won my game by 13 points. The people at Simla are treating our fellows much better than in other parts of India. There is a skating rink , picture house and theatre at Simla. The people use rickshaws to go about in instead of gharries owing to the steep hills.

May 22nd - the jackals and cheetahs make an awful noise around the bungalows at night, and a cheetah came into our bungalow the other night.

May 23rd - wrote letters. I hear that the Londons are going up to tank on the frontier as the Maksuds are getting a bit saucy.

May 24th – played billiards against no1, lost my game by 40 points.

May 27th – played billiards again. I won my game by 47 and our team is now top of the league.

May 28th - received orders to mobilise all men, and officers on leave have been wired for.

2:30pm - Medical inspection at the hospital. I believe we are going to the frontier.

May 29th – lecture on our work as signallers on the frontier. Kitted out with new boots and short Britishwarm coat.

May 31st - inspected by the General. I played billiards against no 11 platoon and won my game by 27 points.

June 1st – they don't seem to be in a great hurry to move us, I suppose at the finish we shall not be wanted. Went to Ben Storey's pictures.

June 2nd - 9th – Parades as usual.

June 10th – Jesse and Allen gone to the 46th Brigade section at Lahore.

June 11th – I hear that a lot of sick and wounded are coming here from tank. The Gurkhas got into a rather a mess on the frontier – they lost some machine guns and a lot were killed. We are moving again, this time to Ferozepore, one of the worst stations in India. We have put our foot in it this time. I wish we were going on Surries.

June 12th - inspection by General, had photo taken.

June 14th – packing up. Some of the Queens Regiment arrived here today from tank, they look about done.

June 15th – we leave here tomorrow. I am rather sorry to leave as it is a very decent place with quite an English climate. The scenery is also very nice and on clear days one can see the river Surtly about 30 miles away down on the plains. The snow hill near Simla look very pretty in the sun and in the background rise the great snow clad Himalayas, to about 20 to 25 thousand feet.

June 16th – 5:20pm – Left for Durhampur station on the Kalka – Simla railway station in a heavy thunderstorm. We got wet through before we had gone halfway.

7pm – left for Kalka. The view from the train is fine, the railway winds in and out and round the hills. It is like being on the scenic railway, and several of the fellows were ill through the motion of the train.

10:30pm – left Kalka. It's very hot here, I should say well over 100 degrees. Ferozepore is about 200 miles distant.

June 17th, 8:30am – arrived at Ferozepore and had breakfast outside the station. It is very hot here, the sweat pours off one when sitting down, I don't know what it will be like when we start marching.

11:30am - marched to the barracks about 3 miles with packs, the temperature being 109 degrees in the shade. The doctor stopped us and told the Colonel off for bringing us up in the heat of the day. Several fellows fainted when we arrived at barracks.

June 18th - did not sleep much last night as it was too hot. There is a breeze going today so we don't feel the heat so much. We have to help garrison the fort here.

June 19th - 5:30am: signalling parade until 8:30am. After this we do not have anything to do as it is too hot.

June 19th – there is a picture palace run by the Sussex Regiment here but the pictures aren't worth seeing.

June 20th – as usual – we have native cooks here so the food is better than it has been in the past.

June 24th – very hot today, spine pads have been issued out. There are about 50 fellows in hospital with severe heat stroke etc. Went down to the Sunan bazaar in the morning. We sleep with just a sheet on us and this is wet through with sweat by the morning.

June 25th – we get physical drill in the bungalows from 10am to 11:30am to prevent us going to sleep.

June 26th - 29th Usual parades, there isn't much to see in Ferozepore and one isn't allowed into the city. This is a Sikh stronghold and it is near here where a big battle was fought between the Sikhs and the British. Amritsar is their holy city and is not very far from here. It is noted for its golden temple. It is certainly very pretty, but nothing as grand as the Taj Mahal or the Jumma Masjid at Delhi. Our regiment is doing guard at the fort here.

June 30th – temperature 115 degrees today, too warm to write much.

July 3rd – raining hard today, we had a route march out to the fort towards the river. The river is crossed by a very fine bridge near the city which has a road track with a railway beneath. It is about a mile long and called the Kaisar 1 hind bridge.

July 5th - I am going to Kasauli on a signalling instructors' course tomorrow with G Kingsworth and Lionel Hodges.

July 6th – going tonight. I am very glad to get away from this place. We are going for three months.

6:20pm left Ferozepore, travelling first class.

July 7th, 6:30am – Kalka. We had a decent journey up and travelling 1st class we had a decent place to sleep and electric fans. We shall have to walk to Kasauli, which is nine miles up the hills at a height of 6000ft.

12 noon – Arrived at Kasauli, which is beautiful and cool. It

doesn't seem possible for the temperature to alter so much in a few miles, although it is the altitude which accounts for it. Hodges has gone into hospital with malaria. he was feeling ill coming here in the train.

July 8th – we are in bungalows here and it is fairly comfortable. We start our course on Monday. The monsoon weather is here now and it rains every day.

July 9th - Sir J Munro, the CIC, inspected the station this morning. Had a look round the place today - it is a bigger place than Dagshai and has many nice walks, the upper and lower mall being the most important ones. There is a soldiers' home, RC Institute and army canteens here. The first seventh Hants are doing garrison work here. The Pasteur Institute for India is here and cases are sent from all over India and even Mesopotamia. Amballa on the plains can be seen from here, also Simla further up, about 60 miles away by road.

July 10th – reading tests today, I got on all right.

July 11th – we get parades from 6:30am till 8pm, so our time is quite occupied.

July 13th - clouds are very low today, we cannot see the hills around us.

July 14th – played hockey for signal school against gym staff. Had a long walk round Kasauli. There is a place here called Ladis Grave where a woman during the mutiny tried to ride her horse down the cliff when she was being pursued by Indians. However her horse fell and both were killed. The spot where they fell is occupied by two graves supposed to contain their bodies.

July 20th - received letters. The view of the clouds which are over the plains below us was beautiful today.

July 21st – August 4th: Parades as usual.

August 4th – walked to Dagshai and after about 24 miles saw some of our fellows there. Some convalescents who were going down to the plains had a row with natives at Kalka and I hear one of our fellows was killed. Troops from Kasauli had to go down there in the pouring rain in the night to make things quiet again.

August 9th - read mail. Lionel Hodges has to return to the Battalions.

August 22nd - went out to Sanawar on a scheme. There is a boys' and girls' school there for Giphams (soldiers' children).

August 24th - signalling scheme to Pine Woods, Barr, Temple Hill, Gibbet Hill, Bazaar Hill, Sanawar Fair, Elfin Lodge and Palpitation Hill.

August 25th – read letters and answered them.

August 27th – out on a scheme from 7am to 3pm. Ins. Adams and Ins. Ossling, two of our subs, are here on this course.

August 30th - short theory examination.

Sept 2nd - I hear that 160 of our regiment at Ferozepore have joined the 6th Hants for Mesopotamia.

Sept 3rd - had class photo taken.

Sept 6th - hear that two of our fellows have died at Ferozepore, Sgt Lillywhite and Pettit of my old platoon. We get some glorious sunsets here, the clouds sometimes are about 1000ft below us and stretch as far as one can see. It looks like level country covered in snow, which as the sun goes down gradually turns to a beautiful pink colour. Sometimes there are holes through the clouds through which one can see the plains over 6000ft below. The effect is usually caused by the monsoon weather.

Sept 7th - 15th — we had a preliminary reading test. I got top of the school in the first and tied for second place in the second. I also tied second in preliminary map reading test paper. The weather is cold.

Sept 23rd - raining hard today. It has been raining on and off nearly every day since we arrived.

Sept 24th — started our finals today. Our finals consist of small flag test, buzzer sending, lamp reading test, telephone exchange test, large flag sending, cable laying test, lamp sending, small flag sending , telephone tracing faults, map compass and protractor tests, buzzer reading, helio sending, helio reading, helio setting up and aligning, exam paper on signalling, exam papers on telephony, exam paper on map reading, taking a squad at flag drill.

Sept 24th–Oct 6th - final exams. I think got on all right.

Oct 7th - we are going down tomorrow, we have had a fairly decent time up here and the instructors were decent fellows, especially Sgt Martini DCM.

Oct 8th - said goodbye to the fellows who aren't coming our way and left for Kalka 2:30pm.

7pm - leaving Kalka for Ferozepore. Stopped at Amballa, where I saw Mr Hawthorn. He came across to say goodbye.

Oct 9th — 9:20am -Ferozepore once again, the weather is nothing like as hot as when we left in July.

Oct 10th - we have a holiday until Monday. The fellows here look very pale and there are a large number in hospital. Nearly all officers are away.

Oct 11th - the nights are getting quite cool now and the evenings are perfect.

Oct 15th - put my name in for wireless operator job in RYC with George and Lionel.

Oct 16th - started firing on range. I started classification test straight away without doing my instructional test as I wanted to get it over in case I was wanted by the RYC.

Oct 18th - finished firing on range. I managed to get a marksman. Heard result of our instructors' course at Kasauli - I got a distinguished certificate. There were only 4 distinguished certificates given on the course out of 100 fellows so I didn't do too badly. George also got a D.

Oct 19th - instructing squad at signalling.

Oct 21st–Nov 5th - out with squad etc.

Nov 6th - all the Battalion are entrenching near here.

Nov 8th - I hear that we shall be wanted by the RYC, so expect to go in a day or two. The Kents have arrived here. I hear that our Battalion is to be mobilised. Wrote letters home.

Nov 9th - Battalion still digging trenches to practise trench warfare.

Nov 12th - have received orders to be ready to move to the RYC at any moment.

Nov 15th - an aeroplane is coming over tomorrow to take photo of our trenches.

Nov 16th - Inoculation at hospital.

Nov 17th - arm rather stiff today. I do not feel exactly lively.

Nov 19th - laid telephone line to A company camp 7 miles away.

Nov 20th - I and George and Lionel are going to Karachi tomorrow en route for Mesopotamia, where we have to join the RYC. Karachi is about 800 miles away the other side of the Sind desert.

Nov 21st - heard that Gen Maude is dead.

Nov 22nd, 5am - turned out and said goodbye to the boys of

the section and left for the station in the armoured car. The adjutant and Mr Adams came down to the station to see us off, also Dick Carute.

6:40am – Left Ferozepore, arrived at Raewind at 8:20am. Had breakfast and caught the Karachi express at 10:29am.

1pm – Montgomery had dinner on train. We are travelling first class, so are having a comfortable journey.

5pm – we are now on the Karachi side of Multan. It is very dusty and barren about here as we are now about halfway across the Sind desert.

Nov 23rd – had a good night's sleep and past wrecked carriages from the train smash which occurred a week or so ago. 10am arrived at Karachi. In the rest camp now we have a nice little room on the end of the bungalow. Had a stroll around in the evening and visited the pictures. Karachi seems rather a nice place, more like Bombay.

Nov 24th – we have been told that there will not be a boat sailing until next Thursday so we shall be able to have a little holiday. Lost my belt with 35R in it. Had dinner at café and also tea. visited the YMCA.

Nov 25th – hired gharry and drove round Karachi. I saw the building in Bunder Road which collapsed yesterday – about forty people were killed and the natives were digging people out while we were there. Saw the Port Trust general hospital near docks – it is a very fine building. Met Mr Spurling at Howard's rooms, went to Trinity Church this evening.

Nov 26th - had a gharry out and went to Kiamari (The port for Karachi) to see the embarkation officer. Some fellows of the DLI and the Kings are here on the same job as ourselves and there are some of the Somerset LI, West Ridings and 1st Sussex to come. Had supper at the Café Grand and afterwards went to the pictures at the Emperor. Saw the sea for the first time since leaving Bombay in Feb 1916.

Nov 27th - wrote letter home and to Ferozepore.

Nov 28th - drove round Karachi in a gharry, went to the gardens and the zoo and saw the play. General post at the Palace here this evening. Had supper at Café Grand and got back to the rest camp about 1am.

Nov 29th - saw Capt Spurling (Late 9th Hants chaplain) and had a talk with him. 5pm - just been warned to be ready to go tomorrow morning at 5:15am. Packed up.

Nov 30th - 4am, turned out and finished packing. 6am - caught the train for Riamari.

10am - on board the SS Barpeta, a boat of some 7000 tons. They put a lot of Indians chained together on the boat before we came on. They are evidently being taken to Mesopotamia as coolies etc. When we got on board we found that we were expected to sleep on the same deck as the Indians - this we refused to do, so after a lot of argument the captain allowed us to sleep on the saloon deck.

12 noon - moving out of harbour. I hope I have seen the last of India. I am leaving on Mother's birthday, so this maybe a good omen.

December 1st, 6am – turned out, as the deck hands are cleaning the decks. The sea is rather choppy this morning.

3pm – Sea is nice and calm now we can see the coast to the north of us.

December 2nd – We get Divisions (Boat Stations) every morning at 10am.

December 4th – Getting near the land.

3pm – Took Pilot on board

5pm – Going up the river.

8pm – We have anchored for the night, it is very cold here at nights.

December 5th – Very cold this morning.

11pm – Reached Basra. There is a lot of shipping here, there is a monitor and a light cruiser in the river near here. Passed a large hospital on our left.

2pm – Going on shore in tugs, we are going to the RFC camp at Tanooma which is the opposite side of the river to Basra. We have been put into a hut made of rushes with a floor consisting of dust a foot deep. I expect they took us for niggers. There is a small YMCA place here, but they only sell biscuits and tea and if one goes in a minute after closing time they will not serve you. It is run by the usual Yank (American).

December 6th – Turned out on fatigue moving huts etc. There isn't a wireless place here, so we will have to go to Baghdad.

December 7th – On fatigue from 6am to 1pm and 2:30pm–5pm, but some of the Karauli course fellows who came from Bombay are on the same job as we are.

December 8th – fatigue, went across river Ashar. There is a rather decent bazaar there and a fine YMCA. The shops in the bazaar are much the same as the ones in India and they sell the same class of goods. Chiefly Japanese.

December 9th – An aeroplane came down on top of one of the huts here today. It smashed the plane, but the pilot was only slightly injured. Going up the river tomorrow.

December 10th, 8:30am – Went down to the river by motor tender and went aboard a river steamer. We have the top deck to ourselves, so if it keeps fine it should be an interesting journey. Passed the monitor which did such a good job against the Turks. Its funnels etc are riddled with bullet holes.

December 11th – We are moving at about 3 miles per hour. There is a coal barge either side of the boat which no doubt accounts for our slow progress. It is very cold, so we are wearing our serge and overcoats.

7pm – Arrived at Kurna at the junction of the Euphrates and Tigris rivers. The site of the Garden of Eden is supposed to be here. No wonder Adam and Eve couldn't agree in a place like this.

December 12th – The country is getting very barren now, though there are a few clumps of trees in various places. Two tramloads of troops passed us in open trucks. I should imagine they have a rather a cold time during the night. There is a cold wind going today. Passed Ezra's tomb on the right bank – it is situated in a clump of palm trees. It is like a small Indian temple with a blue dome.

December 13th – Passed a blockhouse, stopped at a camp where a boat bridge is across the river. The 7th Hussars who are trekking to Samarra went over it while we were here.

December 14th – Amara stopped here and we went ashore for an hour or two. Bought various articles at a bazaar.

7pm – Our skipper went ashore and got some Arak (Arab whisky), which made him mad drunk, so he came on board and began driving the boat all over the place. We ran into another boat and smashed our little boat. We then went full speed ahead into a bank and then full speed astern into the opposite one, where we stuck for a while. We called an officer on board here to put the captain of the boat under arrest, but our skipper told him to clear out or get thrown overboard, so the officer cleared off. The boat got clear again and started off downstream once more. There was only a Sergeant on board in charge of us and he was afraid of the skipper. We had by this time got fed up with dashing about all over the place in the dark and expecting any minute to get sunk, so we told our sergeant that we were going to tie the skipper up. So getting him in his cabin we rushed him and tied him up on his bunk. Shortly afterwards some naval police who had been warned came up in a launch and took him ashore. He will probably get three years for his little game.

December 15th/16th – Passed nos. 1, 2, 3 and 4 marching posts, these are for troops who march up. The river banks are high in places and there are a great number of Arab camps along the banks. We have to put guards on every night as the Arabs are fond of swimming up to the boat at night when it has stopped and try to get on board to steal. Navigation is rather dangerous at nights owing to sand banks etc.

December 17th, 5pm – Kut-El-Amara. We went ashore here and stayed at the rest camp. There was about 4" of dust in the tents. Visited YMCA and canteen.

December 18th – There is no washing place in the camp, so we have to go down to the river. Wrote letters. There is a battlefield just below us and there are remains of bones etc. all over the place. The Arabs, jackals etc dig them up.

December 19th, 5:15am - turned out and packed up our kits and carried it down to the river. It was raining in torrents and the dust of yesterday was turned into mud as slippery as glass. We had to wait on the bank in the rain for two hours, and eventually went on board a rather large paddle boat (PS 51) the roof of which leaked like a sieve. We were wet through, also our kit, and there was not a dry spot on deck. To cheer us up a little cold wind came up and nearly froze us. There are hundreds of rats on the boat.

December 20th – the banks are getting high now and there are five or six Arabs running along the bank calling out to us to give them something. They have been running for miles, and one old fellow of about 60 years of age is still running. He has taken off every bit of clothes he had on. To be able to run faster our fellows cheer him on, but I don't think he will get anything.

December 21st-22nd – An officer visiting rounds last night fell off the ship, but a sentry threw him a lifebuoy which he managed to get. The small boat was launched and after a long row he was picked up. The current was too strong to go back so they walked back and we put the steamer in.

December 23rd - passed some old forts. We are getting near Baghdad now, and we shall get there today. Anchored at Lloyds hut YMCA. One of the machine gunners fell off the barge and sank like a stone. Our boat was out there hours looking for him but could not find him. There is a very strong undercurrent in this river.

December 24th – we got off our boat and got in the T10 boat, which took us up to the pontoon bridge Baghdad. The distance from Basra to here by river is about 600 miles. There was no transport about to take our kits or anyone to meet us, so we went into a refreshment place and had dinner. Finding no one turning up to meet us, we got some Arab boys to carry our kits up to the wireless station, a distance of nearly 2 miles. Here we were put into a EP tent, 10 men to a tent.

6pm - we haven't had any food yet and there seems to be

little hope of getting any. Had a rotten stew served out later – it was a case of eat this or nothing, so we ate some of it. This is about the worst Christmas Eve I've spent.

December 25th – Xmas Day. We did not get anything to eat until 2pm and then it was the same stew as was served up last night. Had plain bread and cup of tea , they also gave us an issue of rum which must have broken their hearts. Met Morey Adams in Baghdad in the evening, he is with the 6th Hants who are in camp near here. There is no place to wash here so we go over to the railway and ask the engine driver to let us have some out of the engines.

December 26th – the weather here is better now.

December 27th – visited Baghdad for the day, the streets are very poor with the exception of a new street which runs from the south of Baghdad to the North. The other streets are chiefly bazaar streets, and are very narrow and covered in. There is an Australian wireless station in the city. Heard about Gen Maude's death. He was hated by most of our troops out here, as he used to sign too many death warrants.

December 28th – went over to see the 6th Hants, as a lot of our fellows of the 9th came out here with them from India. I met a lot of fellows I knew - they have to sleep 15 in a tent (160lb) so they haven't a lot of room. The wireless station near where we are camped was the German station which was captured when we occupied Baghdad but Fritz saw to it that he didn't leave anything of use to us. He destroyed everything and on the walls of the building are inscriptions such as "Gott Strafe England"(May God punish England) etc.

December 29th – medical inspection at the hospital. It was the strictest one I've had. The hospital, or rather the place where the doctors hold sick parade, is in a shed adjoining the station (Baghdad West). The station is a very poor place consisting of one platform and a long shed in which is the telegraph office etc. there are some YSMR engines on the line and two or three very large engines which were thrown over a bank when the Turks retreated, but our people got them up and repaired them and now they are going fine. A lot of Turkish prisoners passed through here today - they didn't appear to be at all miserable. They were wearing ragged clothes and a lot only wore sandals on their feet.

December 30th - the food is still very poor.

December 31st – starting work today. Our parades are:

6:30am – physical drill

9–10:30am – buzzer reading

10:30am – 12 noon – lecture on wireless

2pm – 3:30pm do do

4–5:30pm - buzzer reading.

CHAPTER FOUR

1918

Jan 1st 1918 – The balloon section who have been camped near us left today. Our instructor is Sergt Beatty from Farnborough school.

Jan 5th – Raining hard today, the ground is very slippery.

9pm – We had a hailstorm just now - the stones were larger than marbles.

Jan 7th – Wrote letters, still raining hard. The ground is as slippery as ice.

Jan 9th – Theory exam - I came out 2nd of the school.

Jan 11th – There was a raid by Arabs on the station last night. We could hear the rifles of the sentries quite loud, as the station is only 300 yards from us.

Jan 15th - 2nd theory exam.

Jan 20th - 3rd theory exam. We had half the day off so we explored the bazaar in the city. There is one part of the bazaar where natives make all sorts of metalwork. They will make a ring out of a Turkish sovereign in a few minutes. Received letters.

Jan 25th – There was an aeroplane raid here last night. George and I were over the station getting something to eat. When we heard a bomb go off just outside, we rushed out to see what was going on, and we could hear the enemies' machines quite plainly. But it was dark so we couldn't see anything. Meanwhile the alarm gongs were going, also our defence guns including a pom-pom on a monitor in the river. Just as we were going across the railway he dropped a bomb about fifty yards away. When we got back to our little camp we found all the fellows had cleared off and got behind a bund (tank). At 1am Johnny Turk came over again and dropped several bombs, some in the rest camp near us, killing some Indians. He did not bomb Baghdad city as the Turks consider it a holy city.

Jan 26th – Expected Johnny over again, but he was driven back further up the line.

Jan 27th – Theory examination.

Jan 29th – Rumours about Austria giving in, smallpox has broken out in the rest camp.

Jan 30th – Theory exam, I am now 3rd in the school on theory.

Feb 2nd – Buzzer test at 21 words per minute. We visited an Arab theatre last evening. It is situated in one of the main bazaars. We went in and sat down on sort of loungers (without the padding) and after waiting for half an hour the curtain, or rather piece of rag, went up to reveal three girls (Persian) and four men, but before they started the show they had a cup of tea and something to eat, the men lighting up cigarettes. We of course had to sit and watch them. We were getting fed up with this, so we shouted out to tell them to get going with the show, which eventually they did. They started by singing, or at least trying to sing, a song, but from our point of view it wasn't exactly a success. After this a girl sang, but she made a noise like a cat on the roof at night. Following this a girl danced the Persian snake dance, which was very tame compared to what I expected. After she had finished someone in the wings threw some money and flowers on the stage. This was evidently an enticement for us to do likewise, but she was unlucky. She afterwards came down to the place where the people were sitting and sat on a dirty Arab's knee. We four were the only Europeans there. the audience consisted of chiefly Arabs, Armenians, etc.

Feb 4th – theory exam, spent the rest of the day in the city.

Feb 8th - Finals of stations erection and ground strips. Wrote letters.

Feb 9th – telegraphy final exam.

Feb 10th - theory final exam.

Feb 11th – Holiday. George and I are going away tomorrow.

Feb 12th – Received orders to proceed with George and four others to Fallujah, a place on the Euphrates river. Lionel is going to Bagubah on the Diala river and we have been posted to the 30th Squadron. Some have been posted to the 63rd, who are at Samarra. I finished 3rd of the school on wireless theory. Am leaving here tomorrow. I am rather sorry to leave as I have had a fairly decent time here. Still I want to see come scrapping before it's all over, and I look like getting my wish fulfilled.

As I have little spare time I will write "A visit to Baghdad City".

Starting from the old German wireless station near where we are camped we go across the aeroplane to the railway which runs to Samarra (It is of the broad gauge Indian type in places). There are several German engines in the sheds here. We pass the station, which consists of one platform about 80 yards long with one long shed to serve as booking office, telegraph room etc. On the line one noticed several wooden sleepers between the German iron ones, showing where the Turks pulled the line-up when they retreated. We cross the railway and go towards the river. On the way there is a compound where the Turks buried our fellows who were prisoners. Another place where our fellows and Indians who died here during last summer were buried.

Further on we come to the river, which is crossed by a pontoon bridge which opens at certain times for river traffic. If one wishes or the bridge is open, one can get an Arab boy to row one across in a boat for a few annas. Some of the Arabs row about in a coracle, a round barrel affair, made of a kind of rush lined with bitumen.

Once over the bridge we find ourselves in Baghdad and turn sharp to the left about thirty yards past the bridge and into the big bazaar past the YMCA. The scene now becomes completely Eastern, and one notices a great variety of colours worn by the natives. The Arab men usually wear either white or drab brown, while the Armenians chiefly wear European-type clothes with the exception of headgear, which is usually a Turkish fez. One meets various nationalities including Turks, Arabs, Armenians, Persians, Kurds, Jews and various Europeans. This bazaar is covered in, as also is the one running parallel with it. The shops are like the Indian ones and are rather picturesque in places, one will sell coloured bead and necklaces only, which they will hang out all over the front of the shop. The fellow who owns the shop tries to get one to buy, but he is not so persistent as the Indian, nor will he bargain so long. The shops are chiefly owned by Armenians.

As we walk along the bazaar, boys and girls come up and try to sell us various articles such as rings, watches, beads etc. We buy a few articles from a shop, and immediately boys come to ask if they can carry them for you. They usually carry a basket for this purpose.

On every side one can see children who are diseased. Their eyes are truly awful. It is terrible to think of the thousands of children in this state in this city. Our doctors are doing a lot for these children now. Some of the girls about here are very nice looking, as also are the Armenian women. Although the majority of women are made up a lot, they use a kind of blue on their eyes to make them appear bright.

This part of the bazaar is the cloth and silk bazaar. All the shops sell silks, carpets, clothes etc. In one of these shops I heard an officer offer Rs300 for a Persian carpet, but the shopkeeper wanted more.

The next place we come to is a sort of general store where the shops sell all sorts of articles. Many of the Armenians in these bazaars can speak Turkish, French and English. French is very well known here, owing no doubt to the fact that there was a French colony here before the war and also a convent where many Armenian children were educated.

We next explore a narrow alley place branching off from the main bazaar, and go down to where the city metalworkers are making all sorts of metal goods and fancy article to sell in the shops. They will make a ring out of a Turkish sovereign for Rs20. Some of these workmen use quite modern tools. One notices the absence of women down here, with the exception of the lower classes.

Going further along we pass a military hospital where a lot of our fellows are. At the corner of the bazaar is an old man with a bag full of rupees etc. He is a money changer. We now turn into the main street, called New Street. This is a much larger street and contains the chief shops and buildings, Leach and weborney has a place here. The pavement is about three feet above the road and is composed mainly of old bricks and stones.

Further along I go into a hairdresser's for a haircut. The barber is an Armenian. He makes a fairly decent job of it and calmly asks for 1 rupee, however after an argument I gave him just half of what he wanted, which was quite enough. There are photos of Turkish officers etc. in the shop and a German postcard exactly the same as the English ones of the "Great Sacrifice", only the soldier is a German. There is also a large photo of the Sultan.

Going out, we look around for a place to have tea and eventually decide on one where we can go in, and find a rather clean sort of a place owned by an Armenian who brings us tea and bread (chappaties) and butter, cakes etc.

There is a notice on the wall giving a list of all persons employed in the place , and a certificate to say the owner is authorised to sell refreshments to troops. We get into a conversation with the owner he said that the Turks took off many of the Armenian men when they left. He said the Turkish soldiers had no money and everything was paid with paper money, which was considered useless.

As it was getting late we decided to return to camp, first calling in at the YMCA for a few wads (cakes). The women one meets in the streets are Jews, Armenians and Arabs. The Jews wear a kind of shade which conceals the top portion of the face, the Armenians wear a black veil through which one has a faint view of the wearer – some leave one eye exposed. There is a horse-drawn tram which runs between Baghdad and Kadimain, a place to the north of Baghdad where there are some fine temples. There are some really fine buildings or temples in Baghdad city. The biggest mosque is I believe the one in New Street, but this is very inferior to the fine mosques etc. one finds in India. The above description will I think give one a slight idea of what Baghdad city is like under British occupation.

Feb 12th, 4pm – went down to the rest camp (coolies took our kit down). We had to wait about here till early this morning. We spent most of the time in an empty truck trying to get some sleep.

Feb 13th, 10am – arrived at Fallujah on the Euphrates, where a car came to meet us and take our kits to the flight.

6pm - staying at the flight tonight, I am to go up the line to Ramadi to join the 222 Brigade Royal Field Artillery as a wireless operator. I am the only one to go - all the others are staying with the artillery here etc.

Feb 14th - Johnny Turk came over in his plane today but didn't drop any bombs. He came in the afternoon and no one fired at him, so he had quite a joy ride.

Feb 15th - left by Ford car for Ramadi at 7am, reached Ramadi about 10am. The country was very wild and flat on the way. The Brigade to which I am attached are stationed in a clump of trees near the river.

Feb 16th – Getting settled down now. I am in an 80lb tent and am fairly comfortable. This is the front line, but the Turks are a good distance away, so we do not get troubled much except by aeroplanes. Johnny comes over nearly every day to see how we are getting on. We give him a good reception with our guns usually, and he then turns around and goes off back.

We did a reconnaissance towards Hit today and got into action with some Turkish cavalry who retired after a few rounds.

Feb 17th – Our Brigade is getting after the Turks today. Later (4:30pm) we are at a place called Ukbah. We left camp this morning. We have just one change of underclothing with us and one blanket. Hit is about 60 miles further on. The observation balloon is following us up. I understand the 4th Dorsets are about here somewhere. We have been in action with Johnny, but nothing serious. The Herts Yeomanry have taken about 30 Prisoners.

Feb 21st – Very cold this morning. 8.30am started on our journey towards Hit. Stopped about 8 miles from Hit, and just as we were going into camp a Turk came along in a plane and flew along our column, dropping bombs and firing his machine guns. He killed a few Gurkhas who were acting as escort but missed the artillery.

3pm – Johnny came over again and dropped bombs in our lines close to my tent, killing a lot of mules. I could hear the bombs coming down. When the bombs began to come, the fellows had to get our horses off the line. Then the horses stampeded – it was quite exciting for a time. I had as much as I could do to keep from being knocked over by horses.

We can see Hit from the town. It is on top of a hill, and there is a high minaret on one side of the town.

6:30pm – some of our planes have just gone over to give Johnny some bombs in return for those dropped this afternoon. I have heard we are going to occupy Hit and that we go into action tomorrow.

Feb 22nd – eight of our planes are over the Turks bombing and our C Battery has been shelling Johnny to find out his gun positions. Johnny however was too cute, and he wouldn't reply.

Feb 23rd - Our planes have been bombing the enemy all night. The last one to return home sent down 'au revoir' and 'cheerio' on his klaxon horn as he flew over us. A machine gun was firing in the night and the bullets were coming over and around our tent.

The 215 Brigade RFA arrived here today. The food is very poor now, bully and biscuits, and none too much of it. We have 12 armoured cars with us. I hear our Brigade are to retire to Ramadi, owing I believe to lack of transport to bring up our supply of food etc.

Feb 24th – Moved off back to Ramadi. "B" flight RAF have reached Ramadi from Fallujah and they are stationed out near the Ramadi battlefield . There is a monument to the Dorsets, Queens etc. who were killed in this scrap - it is situated close to where the fellows were buried.

5pm – Johnny came over just now but was driven off. There are some very large fish in the river here, some of which weigh 250lbs.

Feb 25th – Johnny over again. He had a scrap with one of our machines which went up after him, but our plane was injured by our own barrage so it had to come down. The SPAD and about a dozen RE8s chased Johnny home, but he got away.

Feb 26th – Moved off further down the river and pitched our camp. We are in the middle of a clump of trees. Fixed my wireless up and took press from Basra.

March 2nd – received letter. A lot of Arab children come round our camp for food and anything they can steal. The Arabs continually said the S and T dup here.

March 5th – Out on a shoot with the Brigade 10am-12:30. There was a terrific dust storm nearly all the time.

My job with the artillery is when in action to fix up my wireless, get into communication with the aeroplane and take enemy positions etc., which I give to the Brigade commander who is firing on that position. I get from the aeroplane the position of where the shells drop so that the battery can alter its range until it gets OK. With this Brigade I work four batteries, 3 of 18 pounder 6-gun batteries and one 4 gun 4.5 battery making a total of 22 guns.

March 7 – Going up the line tomorrow, so I suppose we shall see some fun after all. I hope we go right into it and get it over.

March 8th – Packed up a few things to take with me. I have a Ford car to take myself to the station and it will remain with me until operations are over. Just before leaving I lost a small kit bag containing my best suit of drill etc, some Arab must have taken it.

We are back in our old camping place, from where we retired a short time ago.

March 9th - The Turks have driven out of Hit, they didn't put up much resistance. Slept in the car last night. The nights aren't too cold now, the Turks are retiring beyond Hit.

March 10th – There was an awful smell all over the camp last night, I cannot imagine what it was.

March 12th – Had a hard storm last night and the ground is very slippery. The food is very poor again. The adjutant has given me a small tent so I shall be all right now, most of the fellows have to sleep out. Johnny Turk hasn't been over lately.

March 17th – Going up to Hit tomorrow.

March 18th – We have passed through Hit and are now about 2 miles the other side. The journey up was rather rough. Hit itself is situated on the top of a hill. The houses are made of mud and stone and wood and are built about 40ft above the level of the road and are loopholed. No doubt it was considered a stronghold in the olden days. There is a large minaret on its eastern side. The main Aleppo road runs through the Arab graveyard here. There are several bitumen wells here. Our present camping place was occupied by the Turks a few days ago.

There are some very old fashioned water wheels near here

used for irrigation. They consist of 6 big wheels about 35ft in diameter made of branches of trees, with a tree trunk to serve as a spindle. On each wheel are fastened a large number of earthenware jars at various intervals, and as the wheel goes round by the force of the water (the river) they become filled, and then when they get to the top they empty into a kind of trough which leads into the land for irrigation.

3pm - heavy thunderstorm - the hail was like marbles and the camp was flooded in a few minutes, my tent having over a foot in it.

March 20th – fine today. The scenery by the river is very nice here of a wild variety. Johnny, our old friend, tried to pay us a visit today but was driven off by gunfire.

March 21st – I understand that the 18th Division is coming up to support us. When we meet we will give Johnny Turk fits.

March 23rd – Going further up tonight - we evidently intend doing something this time. I have only a small piece of soap and one box of matches. Goodness knows how long they will have to last me. We move at 11pm tonight, so expect to see some fireworks soon.

March 24th Left Hit at 12:30 midnight. It was a glorious night. My car was behind the column and I wanted to get up in front with headquarters driver (an American). Tried to drive out round the flank but after about ½ an hour's drive we found ourselves miles away from our Brigade and close to an Arab village and not knowing if they were friends or enemies. We turned round and cleared off back as quick as we could. Eventually by fudging our direction by the moon and stars we found the column.

3:30am – arrived near some hills and camped down, we got our tents up and turned in.

March 25th – The whole Division is here now (15th div). I hear we are to make a long march to get in the rear of the Turks' position, they have, so I understand, a very strong position not so very far away. But we will soon have him out of it.

We can hear the Turkish guns going, they are evidently registering. Three Turks came into our camp this evening carrying a white flag. They walked through the camp but wouldn't take their flag down. I suppose they thought someone would take a shot at them if they did.

We move again tonight and go into action first thing in the morning. We are going up to Johnny's main position and not round him. Our armoured cars were going round to stop them retiring too fast.

9pm – standing by to move off. Some of the batteries have left, also come cavalry. We are going to march all night and take the Turks by surprise.

March 26th – 6am - hearing the Turks now. Our infantry are getting into action with the advanced position of Johnny.

7am - standing by now waiting the order to advance. Some

THE MESSENGER

of the Dorsets are here. We are all merry and bright. Johnny is firing his long-range guns trying to find us, but we are in a hullah and his shells are dropping 100 yards to our right so we don't care.

4pm – am having a few minutes rest. This is the first minute's rest since 7:20am. We have advanced about 5 miles today, taking two positions, and I am now banging away at his main position which is on top of a long hill about a 1000 yards away. The shells are coming over fairly lively now, and I nearly stopped a packet on my arrival here, two fellows being knocked out close to me.

5:20pm – still in action and getting Johnny Turk groggy.

9pm – have taken the Turks' position. I am now turning in for a little sleep by my instrument (wireless) as I am too tired to write more now. It was a fine sight to see us going into action as fast as the horses could gallop - we had to go across a plain about a mile wide in full view of the Turks.

March 26th – our guns smashed the Turks' trenches to bits, it was hell for them. Going after the rest of the Turks, who are retiring in disorder. We have captured I believe about 5000 prisoners and nearly all their guns.

Later – standing by. We have captured all the Turks who retired and our cavalry and armoured cars are in chase of Johnny's wireless car, which has Col Tennant a prisoner

We have occupied Anah. Here we found huge stores of ammunition etc. hid in caves etc - this we blew up.

The place where the final scrap took place is called Khan Baghdadieh. Anah is about 230 miles by road north west of Baghdad . The long-range guns Johnny was using were taken off the cruiser Breslau.

March 27th – nothing doing today. I had a stroll round to try and find something worth taking home, but the infantry or cavalry had been there before us. There are several German officers amongst the prisoners - they keep themselves apart from the Turks and they seem quite saucy, but they will soon get that knocked out of them. The Turks were very poorly dressed and looked absolutely fed up - some of them were wearing sandals. All the wounded Turks were sent down the line in Ford cars - they seemed to enjoy the ride. Hundreds of little ponies were captured. I cannot understand how these ponies pulled the guns over these hills. I think the Turks have 8 ponies to a gun. We caught some and rode them over the battlefield.

March 28th – had a bathe in the river today, the water is getting warm now. The view down by the river is beautiful by moonlight. There is an island in the middle of the river and the remains of an old bridge which evidently used to stretch across the river here.

March 29th – our armoured cars have recaptured Lt Col Tennant, he was being taken to Aleppo by Arabs. The cars only caught them after going 200 miles up the river. These cars shot down a lot of Turks on the retirement, and Turks' horses etc. were all along the road.

March 30th – Rotten dust storm today, we have the wireless up and can get press from Basra fairly loud. The country around here is very wild. We are at present up in the hills.

I shall be glad to get some decent food. We have been living on bully and biscuits for five weeks and I am about sick of it.

March 31st – General Brooking (CMDQ 15th Div) made a speech at a church parade held in honour of our victory. He said there were more prisoners in this scrap than in any other scrap in Mesopotamia.

April 1st – there was an awful storm here last night and this morning, the worst I 've ever experienced. I was awakened by the tent falling in on me and immediately afterwards the wireless pole fell on top of the tent. After a struggle I managed to crawl out with only a shirt and white shorts on. The rain was pouring down and the wind was so strong that one had to practically crawl against it. The other fellows by this time had got out & we tried to get the tent up again, but the wind was too strong, so we gave it up and made a bolt for the tent where the Affie corporal sleeps, but no sooner had we got inside when that went over. We tried to get this one up again but couldn't do it.

All the tents including the officers' were now down, so I went over to our Ford car and found the driver sat up in front sound asleep - he was the driest man in camp. We had nowhere to go for shelter so we made the best of it in the open until daylight, when the wind dropped and the rain stopped. The cooks then tried to make a fire to make tea and after some time succeeded . We were half dead with cold but the hot tea did wonders.

11am: moved off down into the valley, where it is more sheltered.

April 3rd – packed up. We are going back to Ramadi. I have been out of cigarettes for some time, but the fellow with me has some papers so we borrow some tobacco occasionally and make a few.

Reached Sahila and stayed the night. We have to walk as my car is gone and the roads are very soft so they won't let fellows ride on the guns etc.

April 5th: arrived at Hit and stayed the night.

April 6th, 8:30am - marched all day and reached Mud Fort after walking through loose sand all the way. It started raining just after we got here. Staying the night here.

April 7th – 8:30am - moved off to Ramadi, which we reached in the afternoon. The roads today were awful. The rain had made the sand into bogs and one's feet sank in at every step. I was absolutely fed up by the time I reached Ramadi. We have marched well over 60 miles over loose sand etc. In the last three days.

April 8th – In our old camp again. It is nice to be back here once more and have bread to eat again. The river is in flood now, and a part of the pontoon bridge was washed away today.

April 11th – some gifts arrived today from the ladies of Jubbupore. My share consisted of 1 packet of biscuits, tin of sardines, shaving soap, 60 cigarettes, writing pad, 1lb of sweets.

April 12th – moved down the river a mile or so to what I expect be our summer camp. My tent is close to the river. Received letters - they are the first I've received since leaving Baghdad.

April 15th – it is getting warm now, the river is fine for bathing although the current is very strong.

April 17th dust storm and rain.

April 18th – very stormy, read letters.

April 19th – the other fellow who has been with me on this station has been recalled to the flight. I suppose they will send someone else later on. I have the tent to myself now so have plenty of room.

April 20th – had a terrible night again last night. The rain poured through my tent like a sieve and also came under the sides and there was a foot of water in places. I had to go outside and dig a hole to drain some of it off. My bed, being on the floor, also got covered in mud and water.

April 21st – warm again today, just right to dry my things.

April 22nd - this is a fairly good position for wireless, I can hear Constantinople, Damascus, Eiffel Tower, Massua (Italy), Bucharest, Berlin, Nauen, Berastopel etc. I can also hear nearly all the Turkish field stations. I can read German press from

Nauen and Turkish press from Constantinople every evening.

April 25th – the river is rising owing to the recent storms. There is a lot of thunder about also, but not least plenty of mosquitoes, sandflies etc.

April 28th – the days are getting warm now although the nights are still cool. Food is very poor and we cannot get anything from the canteen.

April 29th – George left for Baghdad today, wrote letters. Basra has increased his speed in sending press lately, he sends at 28 yards per minute now and it makes one sweat to read him.

The Arabs who draw the water close to me have awful voices. They talk to each other across the river and shout to the village about a mile away. When I am taking press one of them usually starts shouting, which makes reading Basra impossible.

May 1st – the weather is getting hot now and I am trying to get another tent to put over this one as a single tent isn't safe during the summer.

May 2nd – had a storm last night, it blew my aerial down also poles, and nearly had my tent down. I had to get up in the night to hold up one of the poles supporting the tent.

I have made a charpoy (bed) today out of some poles and wire. It is fine after sleeping on the ground for so long. The last time I slept on a charpoy was in India.

Concert at 395 battery by the Londons and Sussex rgts. concert party from India, they are touring Mesopotamia.

May 3rd – the flies are beginning to get lively, there are millions about. I shall be glad when I get a mosquito net, so that I can have some peace. The mosquitoes and sandflies are about in thousands during the evening.

May 4th – Horse races near Jacksons' house, and the band of the 1/5th Gurkhas played here this evening. They are very good.

May 6th – cold and rainy today. It is very hot one day and very cold the next. Read letters.

May 7th – I am about £6.15 in credit since arriving in this country, about equal to a week's pay of some ex tramps who are in munition works at home. The R.E.s are trying to get a pontoon bridge across the river here, but the current is too strong. Monitors go by here most days. They have been changed into cargo boats.

May 8th – Have to wear spine pads and helmet shades all day now. Indian leave has started, but I don't suppose I shall get any. As a matter of fact I'm not keen on taking any.

May 9th – have rather a headache today.

May 10th very warm today, although there is rather a nice breeze from the river.

May 13th – Mr Twiner, the adjutant, is trying to get me an E.P. tent for the summer.

May 15th – Inoculated today (TAB).

May 16th – very hot again. I am about fed up staying under this single tent. A lot of fellows are going sick with dysentery.

May 18th – My birthday. Hope I shall be home on my next. The heat in this tent is terrific.

May 19th – spoke to adjutant about a tent, so he has had another put over my old one. It is a lot cooler now. The news from France is bad - still we are bound to win in the end. Read 10 letters from England.

May 21st – there has been an order issued for more economy in food. If they stop any of our present rations they may as well take the lot. Our rations are quite poor enough now.

The police (military) caught an Arab today who is supposed to have stolen things out of our cookhouse. A Persian went into the village disguised as an Arab and caught him with the help of the police after sticking a bayonet into him.

May 23rd there is a rumour going round that Johnny Turk has occupied Anah - still he is quite safe there. A scaffold has been erected in the square at Ramadi where we hang Arabs for looting etc.

May 24th – received gifts from the women of Bombay.

May 25th – Our Brigade concert party gave a show last night, it wasn't great but it passed an hour or two away. The pontoon bridge is in working order.

May 26th – a fellow was drowned in the river here today. He was washing clothes and slipped in and didn't come up again owing to the undercurrent. A fellow named Templeton has just joined and he is just out of England. He plays for Glasgow Queens Park.

May 27th — the Arabs have been trying to get camels across the bridge all day but the camels take some getting on to the wood planks - they have to practically carry them on. One old Arab couldn't get a camel on, so they stuck a knife through its nose and put a rope through and then pulled until he pulled the flesh away. Another Arab knocked a camel's eye right out with a stick. They appear to have no pity.

May 28th - I have an E.P. tent now, so I shall be all right for the summer.

May 31st - rotten news from France. There are plenty of troops in India and elsewhere who would like to go to France. We shall get Fritz groggy, yet the only thing is to fight on till we do. Anyway we cannot lose, I would rather be wiped out than go back to England defeated. Still, defeat never enters our heads.

June 2nd — another of our fellows was drowned here today. He fell off the pontoon bridge. I and another went out in an Arab's boat and two others swam out, but he was gone before we could get to him.

June 3rd — better news from France. The 75th Heavy Brigade arrived here today, Clements and White being with them.

June 7th — the Arab who was caught for stealing got away from his guards and came into our camp last night and tried to knife our Persian interpreter, who was responsible for his arrest.

June 9th – pictures last night in the open. The picture shown last night was the Battle of the Somme. This is the last sort of picture we want, but it is the army way of doing things.

June 11th – wrote letters.

June 13th – YMCA is open now and one can get tea and biscuits there. We are trying to get up a cricket and football team here as playing will relieve the monotony a little.

Pictures tonight, this time the Battle of the Ancre. We want comedies etc., not battle pictures.

June 15th – rather warm today (105 degrees). We were issued with railway cigs. They can be bought in India, about 10 per lamma.

June 16th – Pictures, comic ones this time.

June 18th – The Divisional concert party gave a show last night – they were very good.

June 19th – rather hot today, about 119 degrees in the shade. The river is falling rapidly now, leaving mud banks in the middle of the river. I send a press communiqué each day to the YMCA REs , Balloon Section, to HQs, 1 each to our four batteries and 1 to ammunition column.

June 21st – very hot wind today, these hot winds blow from the Arabian desert.

June 25th - the cavalry have captured a Turkish patrol near Hit. If they get too saucy we shall have to teach them manners.

June 29th - very hot now. We simply lie down all the day and dream of Blighty.

July 1st – received parcel and letter from home. Temperature 123 degrees in the shade. There is no air and it is to say the least warm. I put a wet towel on my head during the afternoon to prevent headaches. The hottest time of the day seems to me about 4:30 to 5pm. The sun is then at a lower altitude and all its power is on the single side of the tents, whereas during the middle of the day it only strikes the top of the tents, which are double.

July 3rd – it is surprising the amount of tea drunk by us during the day, we usually drink 7 or 8 pints per day. I think it does one good as it replaces moisture lost through sweating and it makes one sweat more, which is healthy. We play cricket most nights now.

July 4th - writing this at midnight while listening in for Turkish stations. There are thousands of insects all over my little table and myself. They include mosquitoes, sand flies, small ants, large ants , a kind of earwig, beetles (flying), dragonflies etc. These little things will persist in trying to get into my ears, mouth etc.

July 6th – have got rather a bad cold today. Received letters from Sid G, Sid

Farah and Jack. The old battalion are at Amballa with some at Kasauli.

July 9th – the E.T. canteen has sold out all its goods so we have to live on army rations only now.

July 15th – very hot today, the shade temperature has reached 124 degrees. The evenings aren't too bad. I don't think we shall get much more fighting out here as Johnny Turk is as fed up as we are of this godforsaken country.

July 17th – Winnie's birthday, hope she is having a good time.

July 18th – there is an order out prohibiting any sports being held and no work to be done between 8am and 6pm owing to the heat. Basra usually send his press out at 5am now.

July 19th – the Arabs are getting thousands of camels across the river here, I think they are to serve as our transport as I hear we are going up towards Aleppo across the desert.

July 20th – better news from France today, our people are on the advance again. I hope they keep it up, about time this little war was over.

July 24th pictures this evening, or at least they tried to show them but the machine broke down. We get issued with two bottles of soda water every day, it is more like dirty water than anything. They also issue us with guava jam – it makes one ill to even look at it. The Arabs in the villages charge 4 or 5 annas an egg (fowls). They are very small.

July 25th I see in Reuters that some of the munition workers are on strike in England. Some of our boys would like to get amongst them with their bayonets, they would soon decide to work then.

July 30th - good news from France.

August 2nd - Arabs who draw water near here sing and shout all night, keeping us awake. I feel like shooting them some nights.

August 6th - Basra hasn't sent any wireless news for 6 days, there must be something doing in France. I take the German press sent out by Basra and Nauen and it points to our still advancing.

August 7th an epidemic of influenza has broken out here. A lot of the Dorsets have got it. We have to gargle out throats night and morning. A lot of our fellows are ill with fever etc.

August 8th – played football against 1070 battery, we beat them 3-0. Received letters. Some of the fellows are back from Indian leave - they look rather pale and say the Indian authorities treated them very badly. Some of them had to stay in the depot in India all the time.

I hear that Whittaker of A company has died at Amballa.

August 10th - played footy, we won 3-0.

August 12th - hotter today. I shall be glad when the time for operations comes along, I would much rather be scrapping than sticking here in this heat. Played footer against Kites Balloon sections, we drew 2-2, it was very warm. We play in the evening. The insects are a nuisance at night and it is a job to go to sleep. The trees are big with dates now, although they are not fit to pick yet, these trees belong to Arabs and they pay our people 1/- per tree tax.

August 20 - played football, drew 0-0. A party of Germans have escaped from Baghdad - they have some journey if they want to get back to their lines.

August 21st - going out on a practice shoot tomorrow.

August 24th - no press from Basra yet, shoot from 5:45am to 8am.

August 25th - there are rumours going about we are going to Persia to join the Armenian army which is being formed. The date winds are here now and they are rather cold at night. There are hundreds of big scorpions and spiders about and they sometimes get into our beds.

August 26th - Basra has started sending press again, he is on a 3000 meter wavelength now. Cholera has broken out at a place near Debban about 30 miles down the river. Good news from France, we have evidently got Fritz groggy at last.

August 31st - out with 1070 battery on a shoot the did some good shooting getting 0.15m on the fourth shot

Sept 4th - out with Brigade on a Popham panel shoot with the Dorsets.

Sept 5th - Going down to Bills at 395 Bty to support one of the wireless fellows there. He makes good puddings etc. so I often spend the evening with them.

Sept 9th - out with 375 battery on a practice shoot.

Sept 11th - I hear that our "B" flight are going to Persia but that operators on artillery stations are to remain here and be transported to 68 Squadron. An officer from GHQ has been round inspecting stations etc and going out with us on shoots - he is making a report on all stations.

Sept 15th – our officer from Bagubah has been to see me. He told me they were very pleased with my work and that my name has been sent for promotion.

Sept 16th – B flights wireless officer and Charlie came down to say goodbye as they are leaving here tomorrow. I should have liked to go with them, but they had orders from headquarters to leave us. I had the best report amongst the operators with artillery on the Euphrates front, and I am the first for promotion.

Sept 17th – Templeton's birthday was yesterday so we had a feed consisting of two roast chicken, custard pudding etc.

Sept 18th – good news from France. I wish they would send us to help things on a little. The Bulgarians have also had a stoking up. They have asked for an armistice, so I hear, but don't believe it as I have had nothing through on wireless about it.

Sept 29th – Bulgaria has packed in at last, now for Johnny Turk. I had quite a crowd around my tent waiting to hear if it was true.

Oct 1st – Basra sent out in English, German and Turkish that Damascus has fallen with 7000 prisoners. I heard Damascus working yesterday, evidently for the last time.

Oct 2nd – took charge of 74th Heavy Brigade station on a shoot before the General. I had to work the whole shoot with two aeroplanes by myself as the operators on the batteries could not get signals.

Oct 3rd – out with the heavies again. The adjutant of the Brigade said he was very pleased with the way I took the whole shoot yesterday, as if I hadn't been able to take both planes the shoot before the General would have been a failure.

Oct 4th – the flight gave me orders to take charge of Divisional headquarters wireless and leave my Brigade, but the Brigade Colonel wouldn't let me go and saw the General and got me to remain. I'm not sorry as I am quite comfortable where I am.

Oct 5th – pictures this evening.

Oct 6th, 9:30pm – got orders to pack up my station as the Brigade is moving. I think there is something doing on the Tigris front. I have to go by motor convoy tomorrow morning to Debban.

Oct 7th – did not get any sleep last night. I had to get my station packed up etc. When we arrived at supplies at 4:50am it was quite dark and I had to carry a lantern to show the mules who were pulling our kit the road. After staying here about 2 hours we found that the convoy did not go now, so I rushed about and interviewed the captain of a monitor. As he was going to Debban the next day he said I could go along with him, which we did.

Oct 8th, 5:30am - moved off downstream for Debban and arrived there at 10:30am. I put my station on the bank here, and we could see in the distance our Brigade who were coming down by road. Jock Templeton stayed to look after the station whilst I went off to see where the Brigade were going to camp. After walking three miles I found them at a place called Sheikh Harib. The adjutant said he would send the limber GS down for Templeton and the station.

Oct 9th – this camp is in a filthy condition. It is the camp where cholera broke out a short time ago.

Oct 10th – visited by Mr Bunster and Val. Mr Bunster said my promotion had come through. Reuters today announces capture of Cambrai in France. Basra sent out and told the Turks this.

Oct 13th – there are a lot of Arabs raiding here at night and the sentries are firing every night.

Oct 14th – news from Basra that Germany has accepted Wilson's 14 points, but I don't think our people will let them have peace on these terms. Our terms should be unconditional surrender. If they won't accept that, then carry on till they do.

This is a desolate place to stay in. We are the only white

platoon in the district and there is no canteen here, the nearest is Debban 3½ miles away. The flies are awful here during the day and sandflies are as bad. At night they get into one's bed and it's impossible to find them.

Oct 15th – the runway runs here from Baghdad - it is a change to see trains.

Oct 16th – our fellows are moving forward in Belgium now, Fritz will soon be in a bad state. I have a touch of influenza today so am not feeling too bright.

Oct 17th – the 74th Heavy Brigade are going across to the Tigris front as our people there are moving up to Mosul.

Oct 21st - went up to Ramadi by car to have one of my wireless condensers seen to. Heard Pox (Nauen) sending German reply to Berne (Switzerland). Met Lane at CRA - the 215 Brigade are in our old camp.

Oct 24th – saw the northern lights for the first time out here. They show up like streaks of light (not red as in Blighty) across the sky.

Oct 25th – raining today. Our fellows are fighting hard on the Tigris river. The Turks are putting up a good fight.

Oct 27th – a 4.5m battery has been wiped out on the Tigris when a big scrap was going on and our 429 battery have gone up to replace them. Aleppo we hear has been captured.

Oct 28th – Austria seems on the point of giving in. We are getting on with the war now.

Oct 29th – some Arabs came round my tent last night - they were evidently waiting for me to put my light out. I was listening in for Nauen to send up till midnight when I thought I heard something. I went outside, when about 4 Arabs got up and ran away. It was quite dark so I couldn't see to shoot. The sentry fired at one just afterwards but missed. The YMCA was raided last night, evidently by the same Arabs.

Oct 31st - we have defeated the Turks near Mosul, taking 8000 prisoners and nearly all their guns.

Nov 1st – armistice signed with Turkey. It's about time Johnny gave in.

Nov 2nd – holiday today owing to Turkey's surrender. The Austrians seem in a bad way. Concert by the Brigade party.

Nov 3rd – Reuters states that hostilities with Austria are about to cease.

Nov 4th – news through that armistice has been signed with Austria. Things are looking up - I wonder what Fritz thinks of it now.

Nov 7th – atmospherics are very bad now. It is very hard to read Basra and impossible to hear or at least read Nauen or Eiffel Tower. I listen in for Nauen every day expecting to hear that Germany has given in.

Nov 8th – Germans are retreating rapidly in France. A delegation is reported to have left Berlin for the Western Front.

Nov 9th – there appears to be a revolution in Germany – well, every little thing like that helps to end the war.

Nov 11th – very hard storm last night and the ground is awful today.

10:20pm - have just got it through that Germany has accepted our terms. I am now going to try and hear what Berlin has to say about it. Read letters.

Nov 12th – we are to get a rum ration tonight and there is to be a royal salute and fireworks. How I should like to be in Blighty now. There is no excitement here, the fellows are about fed up. Just after the news came through, if you told a fellow that Fritz had given in he would look bored and say "has he?" in a fed up sort of way.

Nov 13th – Some of the fellows, presumably those who had had some other fellows' rations of rum, went round to each battery commander last night and made them all sing a song or dance. They wouldn't take any excuses. It was very funny to see some of the officers try to sing. All batteries in Ramadi and Hit districts fired a salute of 31 guns.

Nov 14th - weather very nice today. News re the Kaiser being interned in Holland. I hear that my old Battalion, who are in India, are going to Siberia. Applied to squadron for English leave, they replied to say my application is being considered.

Nov 16th - Went over with Jock to see the Arab cemetery across the plain over a large canal. It seems to be a very old one. All these Arab cemeteries are situated on a hill or rise in the ground. The Arabs are buried with their feet towards Mecca, their holy place, and at certain times the women come to the graves and cry and make an awful row.

The Arabs live in villages or camps. The ones who live in camps are the desert Arabs, who are always moving from place to place. There is always a sheikh or head man to every camp or village, and he is responsible to us for the good behaviour of the people under them.

The Arab is a born thief - he cannot resist taking things whenever he gets the chance and they are dangerous fellows to tackle when caught. The best way is to shoot them first and then make enquiries.

The women do most of the work in the fields but in the villages the women seem to decide what they want for eggs, fowls etc. no matter what the men say.

Some of the Arab women are fairly decent looking, but the majority have tattoo marks on their face, wrists, ankles etc. The women are responsible for the village water supply. They come down to the river with animal skins sewn up, which they fill and carry back to the village on their backs. They appear to look after their children very well. All the villages have hundreds of savage dogs about, but most of them are afraid to come very near. In one village however which a friend had entered to buy some eggs, three of these dogs, led by a very old savage brute, came for us so savagely that we had to shoot them off with our revolvers.

Nov 18th - our Brigade team beat the 1/4th Dorsets 2-0 at football today at Debban.

Nov 19th – received letters from Sid Grosse and Jack B from India saying they are going to Russia.

Nov 21st – according to Reuters press, the British Government do not appear to be in a hurry to demobilise us and talk about men whose work is open for them when they go back home. I hope however the Govt. will remember the fellows who came up in 1914 independent of whether they have got a job waiting for them. A man who volunteered should certainly have the preference over a 1917 or 18 conscript.

Nov 22nd - the men have to parade before the doctor every week for inspection for lice. The NCOs are exempt. I never go on them.

They are asking for volunteers for Siberia. What a hope they have! They must take us to be mad. The nights are getting cold now, although still hot during the days.

Nov 25th - received parcel from home. Constantinople has been sending French lately. Evidently the French are working the station.

Nov 26th – have had to give in particulars off our Surries, occupations etc. Demob. Nearly all the late enemy wireless stations have ceased to send now with the exception of Berlin, Nauen, Moscow and Sevastopol.

Nov 28th - the election in Blighty is in full swing now, but they don't seem to want our votes. We haven't a chance to vote. I suppose when we go back we shall find a government put in by munition workers and conscientious objectors, but if they don't act right by the soldiers they will soon be out of it.

The govt. scheme of demob came through today. They are not acting fair with the 1914-15 men and are giving priority to conscripts who have jobs waiting for them. Most of these men have been receiving pay from their employers during their period in the army and had in most cases remained in their jobs until compelled to join, they have therefore been gaining financially all through the war and now they will gain still further by going back before the volunteers. No doubt when the volunteer does get away he will find that the munition workers etc have got his job, or at least all the best jobs going.

Nov 30th – Mother's birthday. Hope she is enjoying herself.

December 1st - A Coy. Dorsets played our 1070 battery at footer. 1070 won 2-1 but I think the Dorsets were the best team.

Dec 2nd - all EP tents are to be handed in to ordnance soon, but the adjutant is trying to let me keep mine. I am the only fellow to have an EP tent amongst the operators about here. They usually give us a small 40lb tent. Have a rotten cold today.

Dec 5th - visited by Lt Denly, our new wireless officer.

Dec 6th – am not feeling too well just lately, this camp doesn't agree with me, I shall be glad when we move.

Dec 7th - I thought I would have a good breakfast this morning, so I cooked some sausages last night and put them on a plate in a box, but this morning I found that a jackal or mongoose had been before me and took the lot. It is starvation here for a fellow not feeling well, the rations are awful.

Dec 9th - had rather an exciting time last night. Some Arabs raided my tent and got away with my boots, tunic, breeches, waterproof sheet and a blanket. One of them was taking the blanket off me when I woke up. He made a bolt and got away before I could get out my revolver. I warned the sentry and we had a stroll around to see if we could see anything of them, but it was very dark. We saw one and fired at him but couldn't take an aim, so he got away.

This evening the political officer and several of our fellows raided the Arab village near here. We had mounted men to keep the Arabs from leaving the village. We searched the village and found three Arabs wearing army clothing, but could not find anything belonging to myself. The three Arabs were brought into our camp and stripped, then tied to a tree and flogged. I am moving my tent to a safer place tomorrow as I'm outside the sentries here owing to this position being good for wireless.

Dec 11th – an Arab was caught by Indians in 1072 battery lines last night.

Dec 13th – attended court of enquiry re my raid. I simply gave a statement of what I knew about it. Templeton has been recalled to Ramadi, chiefly I believe to play football for the flight. Read letters. A fellow named McGuiness has arrived in place of Templeton.

Dec 14th – the Baghdad races are taking place now, the weather is dull and cold. Roll on the Spring and Blighty.

Dec 23rd – went round some Arab villages to try and get some chicken and eggs for xmas. They wanted R5 for a chicken, and eggs were 6 for R1.

Dec 24th – out in the village again for eggs etc. it is very cold in the evenings and nights now, we have to wear our overcoats in our tents after tea. The Handley Page aeroplane flying from Ipswich to India passed over our camp here a few days ago.

Dec 25th – had a fairly decent time today. We each paid about 14/- for extras etc., which consisted of chicken, beef, pudding, fruit and custard. Afterwards we had fruit, nuts, beer etc.

Dec 29th – Mr Moran from B flight Ramadi visited me today. He said I should be recalled at the end of the week as all artillery stations are being recalled. I hear in Reuters that Asquith, Ramsey McDonald, Henderson, McKinna and Co have been defeated at the elections in England. I am glad to hear it, we have had quite enough of them.

Oswald's Unit (Oswald unidentified)

helio work at Dagshei

Indian jugglers

flag drill

American battleship passing Port Said

captured German engine at Baghdad

gun on the Ceramic

CHAPTER FIVE

1919

1st Jan 1919 – result of the elections through. It is a big victory for the coalitionists. I wonder if they will make a better job than the previous ones.

Jan 2nd – B flight 30th Squadron are at Baghdad now. Butter issue has been stopped, we get cheese instead. It doesn't seem possible the war is over, still I suppose it is. We have however shown to the rest of the world and to some of those old fireside prophets that Englishmen haven't forgotten how to fight. The Charge of the Light Brigade was a picture compared to a charge in modern warfare.

Jan 4th - the column gave a concert to the officers of the Brigade and a few friends last night. I was invited and it turned out very decent.

Jan 5th - wrote letters.

Jan 7th – packing up, as I am going back to the flight at Ramadi.

1pm - a tender came for me, said 'bye bye' to the fellows of

HQ. Sergnt Maj Saunders and "Bogey" Campbell asked me to look them up if ever I was in Dover. I am rather sorry to leave the Brigade, as they have always treated me well. I got on very well with the Colonel and also all the officers, many of whom used to call in at my tent to hear the latest news. They never used to interfere with me or my work. The adjutant has asked the flight to send me back to them if ever they are called on for any scrap etc. or practice aeroplane shoot.

We stayed at Debban for some cakes, tea etc. at the Arab place and to get some goods from the EF canteen to take to Ramadi with us. I met Thompson and Davis here. Tommy is going to Baghdad and Davis is going back to Blighty on demob.

Jan 8th – We are now at the flight. Our (wireless) tents are well away from the rest. We have three tents, one to live in, one as an operating tent and the other as a store tent. There are eight of us here and there isn't a great lot to do.

Jan 9th – have started a continuous watch on wireless, we take press from Carnarvon (MUU), Nauen (POZ), Lyons (YN) and Sayville (for New York). These people send English press on continuous wave. Basra and Aden are about the only two sending English press on spark. We can get as much as 24 large foolscap pages each day of press.

Jan 10th – Berlin is continually sending messages to New York groaning about the conditions of the armistice etc. He sends every word twice and very slow

Jan 13-30th - there have been plenty of rumours going about re demobilisation but nothing has occurred yet. Met Sergt Wright of my old Battalion here. He is a pilot in this flight. He got his commission in India. He takes me up for a flight sometimes.

I hear that the natives in the bazaars are raising their prices now that fellows are going home and want to take a few things with them.

Feb 1st - 14th - we get plenty of sport here now in the way of football, tennis , hockey etc. I feel a lot better for it. The Arabs are letting us have eggs, 7 and 8 for R1. I usually eat a rupee's worth a day. Most of the other white troops have gone down the line so we are the only white fellows left, with the exceptions of a few REs and motor transport.

The weather is very nice now, and we can get flights here fairly easily now the planes are chiefly RE8s and one or two DH4s. Some of the other flights consist of SPADs, Camels and SEs.

An Arab strafe is being arranged on a place near Nasariyah below Babylon. I asked to go as an observer but I hadn't any experience with the Lewis gun so I couldn't go.

Feb 18th - I think we are going to Baghdad next week. The Samarra flights are leaving for Baghdad today. The pontoon bridge has been washed away at Debban, so we shall have to wait or else go by river or aeroplane.

Feb 19th - we are getting cold winds here now but haven't

had much rain up to the present. One would imagine that the natives in the bazaar here would sell things cheaper now that most of the troops have gone, but they won't. A lot of the articles they will never sell once we are gone. I think they would rather keep the things forever than sell them to us cheap. Some of the shop fellows came up from Baghdad when we captured the place and these fellows are packing up and going back to Baghdad soon. Most of the shops in the Bazaar here are run by Arab boys. They can talk English fairly well.

Feb 20th - read letters, one of them from Harold to say he had arrived in England from Germany.

Feb 21st – Arabs are being drilled here to act as police guards etc. they have Turkish rifles and they are I believe relieving the Indians for guards.

Feb 22nd – the latest rumour is that all 1914-15 men are going home at the beginning of March. I hope it comes true.

Feb 23rd - McGuiness is going to Baghdad tomorrow, some of our fellows have had release slips. I am however relying on the 1914-15 scheme. There are only five pilots here now, Lt Jacks, Lace, Erans (baby), Wright, and Crighton. They are quite a decent lot. I go down to Jackson's House sometimes and they nearly always ask me to have something to drink etc.

It is quite nice flying now, although the wind is rather rough. The first time I went up it seemed rather strange at first, but I soon got to like it. What surprised me most was the terrific air current, caused chiefly by the propeller. In windy conditions the machine ricks a bit and sometimes gets into an air pocket, when it suddenly drops down through the vacuum to the air below.

Feb 24th – our valves which we use for wireless have been broken, so we cannot take any press now. A memorial to the Dorsets, Queens etc is erected about a mile away, close to the place where most of them were killed. The graves of these fellows are close by and each has a little metal cross with the name etc. of the fellow.

This scrap took place last October when Ramaadi was taken – my old Brigade was in it. They had their positions near Temple Hill. The Herts Yeomanry made a flanking move and cut the Turks' retreat in conjunction with the Hussars etc at Cavalry Hill, which is towards Hit.

Feb 25th – Cold and windy today – looks like rain.

7pm – raining. Mr Lace brought us some valves from Baghdad so we shall be able to take press again. Cpt Valentine has to return to Baghdad, so that only leaves Jacko, Frances, Mathews and myself. We are waiting to be recalled at any moment. We have had an Arab boy named Abdulla who used to clean our plates, knives and forks and keep the tent clean. We didn't leave him in the tent alone much as he wasn't above stealing anything. Once or twice we caught him helping himself to the jam etc.

We have also an Arab dog named Sparky. It is quite a good dog and soon lets us know if any Arabs are about. I always sleep with my revolver tied to my wrist as Arab often try to raid us.

Feb 27th - Jacko (Jackson) left for Baghdad by plane for demob, although plenty of fellows with much less service than myself have already gone home.

March 1st – Val left by plane for Baghdad for duty, so there are only three of us left here now. The life here now is terribly monotonous. The only thing to relieve it is listening in at night for news sent out by various stations. I haven't heard from the fellows I know at Baghdad for a long time now. I don't think they have left, or they would have let me know.

March 2nd – there was an Arab strafe by our plane today below Babylon.

March 3rd – I had a look around the bazaar here today to try and buy a curio of some sort, but couldn't see anything worth having. There are a lot of Turkish watches about, nearly every Arab one meets has one. They want anything from Rs50 to Rs80 for them. An Arab told me anyone can buy the same watch in Constantinople for about Rs15.

March 5th – just read a letter from George K saying he is leaving for England owing to his people getting a release slip through for him. I am making an application to GHQ to see what can be done in my case.

I am getting absolutely fed up with this hanging around, it knocks all patriotism out of one when one gets treated like this.

March 6th – we still listen in from 6pm till midnight for news. Berlin is still moaning about his troubles. Lyons is working with America sending through to NFF - all the news is about the peace conference. This news is sent by the various newspaper correspondents who are in Paris to their papers in America. We get the English point of view from Carnarvon and the German one from Berlin. We can also hear and read Saville, who is close to New York. Some of the other stations we can read are Moscow (MSK), Sevastopol (NKJ) in Russia, Budapest in Austria, Bucharest (BUE) in Romania, Suez (SUE), Aden and Malta, Eiffel Tower in France and many others.

March 7th – moved into the shed at the flight as we have to hand our EP tent in.

March 8th – Arabs came round last night and took a sheep of ours out of the cookhouse. I have another cold coming owing to the changeable weather one day being hot and the next cold.

March 9th – we are going with the flight to Baghdad on Wednesday. I hear Jacko is there still.

March 10th – have been issued with breeches and tunic to replace those lost at Sheikh Habib.

March 11th - the road between here and Debban is flooded and it is impossible to get our cars through. I found an old coin near a cemetery not far from here today – I shall have to take it home, it may be worth something. There was a Ram

Sammy (festival) in Ramadi this evening. They wouldn't let any white fellow in unless he wore some sort of headdress. They wanted one of our fellows to stay the night with them, but a shabaney (Arab policeman) made a motion of his hand across his throat as much as to say if he did they would cut his throat, so he decided to clear out.

The Arab police are acting as guards over our aerodrome now and they are very smart at it. No Arab can get in now, as these police know their little games and can checkmate them. There was a beer issue last night and as usual Val Matheus and co. had a little too much. A favourite game of Matheus when he was a little gone was to take a rifle and ammunition and to go out and look for Arabs. He would let go a few rounds into the darkness and then come into the tent again, saying he had seen Arabs round the tent.

March 12th – have just received orders for Matheus and myself to report to Baghdad for demob. It has come at last, thank heaven. We shall I expect go down to Debban by river and catch the train from there.

March 13th – have got our travelling passes etc. We went down the Jacksons' house to say goodbye to the officers this afternoon and they gave us whisky and sodas etc.

8pm – we are now on board a monitor on the river. We came down in a tender this evening. The boat sails tomorrow morning.

March 14th, 9:50am - left Ramadi for Debban on the F2. I hope I have seen the last of Ramadi.

12:30 – have just past Madjidge. There does not seem to be anyone about here, all the troops seem to have gone. The river has overflowed its banks in several places, but nothing serious. The Arabs' fields will get plenty of water now. The crops etc are looking nice and green now.

There is a Johnny Turk on one of the barges with us – he says he is going to Baghdad to find his bibby (wife). I expect he will have bad luck.

The weather is rather nice today although on the hot side, still I hope to be out of the country before the hot weather starts. There are a lot of Arab camps close to the river. I expect the Arabs are coming in from the desert now that they think we are leaving.

5pm – in the train now. We arrived at Debban to find that the train had left about ½ an hour previous and as only one train goes each day we quite expected to have to stay until morning, but the engine of the train having run out of oil or water it had to return to Debban, so we were in luck.

We have passed Sheikh Habib, where my old Brigade are. They are still in the same place. I hear that SM Saunders and various others have gone home on demob and the Bogey Campbell is going soon.

7pm – arrived Baghdad (South), saw some of the 6th Hants who had come down from Samara, some for demob and some to join the Buffs for army of occupation.

Went out to Baghdad West, which was our destination, and

phoned down to the squadron for a car to fetch us and our kits. I saw Tavey here and slept in his tent for the night.

March 15th - reported to the office and signed various papers. Visited some of the boys who came out with me - I saw Jock, Charlie, Wadhams and Val and several others. Nearly all our old draft are going home for demob on this draft.

March 16th – the Jesters concert party gave a farewell concert in one of our sheds here last night. They were very good, quite the best party I've seen in this country.

March 17th - we visited Baghdad races today and saw the football final for the shield. The MT's beat GHQ 1-0. I saw some very fast tennis in the tennis competition here, wish I could play like it. On our way here we passed large numbers of Arabs etc who were on a pilgrimage, they carried large banners etc. The procession was about a mile long. It has been very hot today, the temperature was well over 100 degrees in the shade. I expect it will be a very hot summer this year, considering the heat already. Read letters and wrote some.

March 18th - As usual. It is about time we heard something about going home, we do absolutely nothing here.

March 19th – I hear we are leaving in a day or two. Medical inspection at the station. I have been paid Rs250, which represents most of my credit.

March 20th – Major Boyd has arrived from Cairo. He flew a DHQ. Capt Babbley and Major Robinson did some rather good stunting today in a Camel and Mono respectively.

March 21st – the food here isn't up to much, one can however get a supper at the Armenian place on the station, otherwise the only other place to get anything is in Baghdad city.

March 22nd – I hear we are to be inoculated against plague. I fail to see the reason for this considering that in India we used to live right amongst it nearly all the year round. The camp here is vastly different to what it was in 1917, there are three squadrons here now, the 30th, 63rd and 72nd beside the wing. There are a lot of Turkish prisoners working at the demobilisation depot here packing things up and cleaning up etc. Some of them quite enjoy themselves and are quite fat.

March 24th - have had our papers checked again. We are leaving tomorrow at 6:45am and going down the river in the same boat (P51) which brought us up in 1917. I'm rather sorry I haven't got a curio or ring from Baghdad. I went down on purpose on Saturday but nearly all the shops were closed so I couldn't get anything.

March 25th, 5:30 am - turned out and packed up.

6:30am - paraded and marched over to the park, to join the Park and Wing drafts. We went down to the boat by tender and got aboard at 8:30am. Three of our pilots flew round the boat and did a few stunts as we were leaving. Major Robinson and Hogan, our wireless officer, came down to wish us luck. Left Baghdad at 10am. The weather is beautiful now - it is rather different to our journey up in 1917.

12:30pm - we are just passing Ctesiphon Arch. This is

supposed to have been the gateway of a large city before Baghdad was built. The country is very barren about here.

7pm - anchored for the night.

March 26th - it was rather close last night and plenty of mosquitoes and sandflies about.

5am - started on our journey again

12 noon - we are getting near Kut now, but I don't think we shall have an opportunity of going ashore.

3pm - Kut-El-Amara. Stayed here for an hour, our people have built a lot of huts since I was here last time. There do not appear to be many white fellows here now.

8pm - anchored for the night. There is a nice breeze blowing now, it should keep the mosquitoes etc away. The weather is glorious.

27th March – beautiful weather again today. Getting near Amara now, the scenery is improving.

4:30pm – Amara. We nearly crashed an Arab boat here as we were getting into the side, there were two men and two women with children in it. The men jumped out but the women only screamed and tore at their hair, calling on Allah etc. The men only just got their boat clear in time to prevent them being smashed against the wharf.

March 28th – have passed Ezra's Tomb. A rather funny incident occurred here - a motor launch passed us and a white fellow was trying to tell our captain something. He stood up and waved his arms about when the wash from our boat struck his launch and pitched him into the river. We of course laughed. He was soon fished out minus his helmet, which floated down the river.

There are a lot of Arabs running along the banks calling out for food etc. There are little boys and girls naked, and one woman took off everything and swam out after a loaf of bread. The river is rather narrow now and we have bumped into the bank several times.

Hope to reach Basra this afternoon. Passed Urnah 6pm, arrived at Margil. We stayed here some time and went ashore and visited a picture house. We are on board now and I am going down to Janooma tomorrow morning.

March 29th – 1pm – I am at Janooma RAF camp now, the YMCA has improved a lot since I was last here. I met Lionel just now and he said George had gone with the previous draft.

March 30th - visited Ashar. We went across the river and up Ashar Creek in an Arab boat (mahalia). I tried to buy some silk, but it was nearly all Japanese and the little Indian silk was two or three times the price one pays in India. Most of the shops are Indian and the Arabs sell Japanese and Indian articles. It is impossible to get any article worth taking home, as there is so much imitation stuff in this country. The YMCA in Palm Gardens is rather a decent place.

March 31st – plague has broken out in Ashar, so no one is allowed there.

April 1st – we have had four inspections of our demob papers since arriving here. The weather is rather warm now. I hope we get cleared out of this country soon. I have been out over three years and have never had any fever or any disease and I don't want to get anything at the last.

April 2nd – we have nothing to do here. I spend most of my time at the YMCA, where one can get tea cakes or read the papers etc. Wrote letters.

March 3rd – going across the river to the demob camp tomorrow, it is getting very hot now and sandflies are about in thousands.

April 4th left Janooma at 7am and went to Magil, where we were fumigated. First we had to put all our clothes into the fumigator, also all our kit in the kit bags. All we were allowed to keep was our boots, towel and helmet. Any valuables we had we took with us in our helmets. We then went into a place and had a bath (cold) of diluted creosote. Then we had a shower bath after drying ourselves – we had a pair of pyjamas and dressing gown. Then we had a cup of hot cocoa while we waited for our clothes to return. When it did arrive we found everything wet through with steam, so we had to put it in the sun to dry before putting it on. The steam spoiled all leather articles which happened to be in the kit bag and I had a pair of shoes and pair of breeches spoilt.

After this little game was finished we went to the demob camp (what a life this is). I met several of my old Battalion here, also Connellan of the 222 Brigade RTA (my old Brigade). The temperature today was 103.5 in the shade, this being rather hot for this time of year. Changed my rupees into English money at the rate of Rs13.5 for the pound – I received £32.

April 5th – the rations here are awful, today our meals have consisted of:

9am tea and small plate of porridge

12 noon tea only

4:30pm tea only. We have to buy all our food at the canteens or else starve. Someone is making a fortune out of us here, and the authorities simply laugh if one places a complaint. One cannot expect fellows treated like this to be patriotic in the future.

April 6th – a large draft are going away tomorrow, we should be on the next one (if we're lucky). Visited pictures at the YMCA, there is rather a decent little reading room towards the river, one of the best I've seen in the army.

April 9th – had our names called out for the next draft which leaves on Friday. Rations are still terrible. It is a shame to issue rations like this, I wouldn't give them to a dog. Still, we are going away, so can put up with the inconveniences now. Wrote letters. We are going on the EKMA. Went through the cage for our final checking.

April 10th - we are not going on the EKMA now as they say it has to be fumigated owing to lice etc. This demob muddle gets on one's nerves. We have been here since 29th of last month. There will be trouble if they do not get us away soon.

April 11th - going tomorrow I hear. Visited pictures at Magil.

April 12th - 4am reveille, 5am paraded and took our kits to a train which takes them down to the boat.

6:30am - on board the Egra, which is about the dirtiest boat I've ever been on. The officers and nurses all have saloon decks. We have the port and aft, which is more like a rag and bone yard than anything else. The nurses were driven down to the boat in motor cars with officers - they look a common lot, I wouldn't be seen with one of them for a fortune. They have a bad name out here. John Bell asked in his paper how it was that nurses receiving so much per month in Mesopotamia could send home about twice that amount.

1:30pm - going down the river now and the weather is perfect. Thank heaven I am out of Mesopotamia at last. I wonder what England is like now. We should be there just in time for the summer. We go to Bombay and trans-ship there.

7pm - have been trying to find a place to sleep but haven't found one yet. The deck is already crowded out with fellows. There are no hammocks or any accommodation for sleeping here.

April 13th - I had to sleep on a heap of coal dust last night, it was the only place I could find. The washing arrangements are awful. There isn't a single bath and there are 1000 troops on board. We shall have to wait until we get to India before we can have a decent wash. Our meals are very poor. Breakfast consists of bread and jam, dinner bully beef, and bread and tea for tea. Could not get on deck this afternoon as it was so crowded.

April 14th - well out in the Gulf now. Passed two ships which dipped their flags to us. The skipper of the boat conducted the church service last night and preached a sermon. He has had a booklet printed about himself. He spoke very well, but if he is the Christian he says he is he ought to make the conditions of the troops better. He could give us one side of the saloon deck if he wished not to let the officers and nurses use it for flirting etc.

Saw King on board, who I knew at Kausali signal school. Rather better food today. The sea is beautiful today and it is turning a blue colour now. It is almost black in the Persian Gulf.

I have managed to find a place to sleep on deck now, it is much better than being below. There are also a lot of rats down below and they run all over one at night.

April 16th - sea is beautiful again today, hope to reach Bombay tomorrow morning.

April 17th – 7am–8am standing by on boat stations as we passed through a mine field.

10am - in dock, Bombay. There are supposed to be two cases of smallpox on board and all troops have to go ashore. The heat is very great.

2:20pm – on shore. I hear we are going to Deolali as there isn't a boat ready for us here. The natives appear to be causing trouble up country.

9pm – our train has run off the line, so we have to stay here I expect till the morning.

2am – had to pack up our bed as the train had arrived.

April 18th – arrived at Deolali – the journey up was rather interesting. The scenery was very fine in places, and we passed through a large number of tunnels. This heat in India makes one sweat so much, in the same temperatures in Mesopotamia one doesn't sweat half as much. Trainload of troops left here for Bombay today, I believe to help put down the native uprising. I expect the white people will treat us like heroes now that they want us to protect them, but when there is no danger they will treat us dogs. I should like to see the natives get hold of the whites and shake them up a bit.

April 19th – the rising seems to be getting serious in various parts, but the natives out here are next to helpless against trained troops. A lot of infantry and artillery are going to Calcutta today. I expect we shall be going somewhere in a day or two. I should like to know why we are being kept here for putting down the uprising. I wonder what the garrison of India is doing, also the much talked of India defence corps (IDF). I suppose they intend staying home while we do the work.

April 20th – some of the Northumberlands and artillery left here for an unknown destination today. They practically refused to go, and some of them fixed bayonets to threaten the officers. A lot of them were too drunk to walk and had to be carried down or taken down to the station in Gharries. I imagine there will be trouble if the authorities keep us much longer, as there is no necessity to return us. The garrison in India are quite capable of looking after a few mad niggers. Our fellows would shoot every Indian they see if it were allowed, as it is owing to the native rising that we are being detained.

April 21st - the papers announce that the troops from Mesopotamia on demob volunteered unconditionally to remain in India as long as they are required. This is an absolute lie - I don't believe one man volunteered. Everyone here says let the whites out here look after themselves, and if the white women are cleared out of the country things would, I think, be much better. They as a rule treat the natives like dirt and the British soldiers as an animal.

April 22nd - visited the picture house at the YMCA. I hear that several of my old Brigade have arrived here.

April 24th - wrote letters. The government of India state that they will pay all the Mesopotamia troops the occupation pay for as long as we are retained. This is useless talk as our paybooks contain an entry to the effect that we have been entitled to it since leaving Baghdad.

April 25th - had a talk to a colonel and staff officers who have been sent down to explain why we are being detained. They gave us a definite promise that we should only be kept one month. We however wanted that statement written in black and white and this they wouldn't do. Some of the fellows told them the white people were not worth fighting for and that they would fight to defend themselves but not the whites.

April 26th – on guard last night over the rifles, my first guard for two years. We being air force we are not supposed to know anything about infantry drill or how to use a rifle, so the authorities are going to send some infantry instructors to teach us as they won't put us on guard until we get proficient in the use of a rifle. This is rather a joke as nearly all the air force fellow here are ex infantry men with service in France or Mesopotamia, but we aren't going to tell them so or we shall get put on guard.

The colonel of the depot here has wired Simba (army headquarters) to hear something definite, as the temper of the troops would not permit further muddling.

April 27th – rather hot today. Several fellows are in hospital with fever and our officer is an hospital with dysentery. There is a very interesting place near here named Nasir which is noted for its Buddhist caves.

Concert at the YMCA run by a fellow named Lupin. The fellows when he was singing kept calling out and asking him, when are you getting into khaki?

April 28th – went to church. This is my first time inside a church since leaving India in 1917.

April 29th - the nights are getting warm now.

April 30th - I hear the demob starts again on May 9th, so with luck we may get away about the middle of May. Visited the pictures last night. They broke down a few times but that is the usual thing out here, we should be surprised if they didn't. One gets very thirsty here in the evenings and I usually consume about 6 bottles of lime juice of an evening. Some medically unfit fellows went through here on their way to England.

May 1st - 4th - as usual. Two women visit the YMCA twice a week to sing to the troops. I wonder if they would do it where there isn't any trouble about? The Indian trouble is practically over now - there were about 600 people killed and about 1000 wounded at Amritsar when the troops fired on the crowds. If any natives near here try any little games they will get a shock.

May 5th – the Colonel made a speech here today which consisted of a message to be read to troops from Simba. He said that we shouldn't talk about being dissatisfied, as the natives would think if they heard us that we shouldn't fire on them if they rose up in rebellion. I think they would be unlucky if they thought that.

A list of sailings from Bombay has been posted. About 8 ships are reserved for troops, so I suppose we shall be leaving soon.

May 6th - moved into another bungalow near the station, I went to a place about two miles away to get my helmet changed but the fellow there would not change it unless it had been condemned by the doctor, so I had to go back and get the doctor to see it. No matter what the state of one's helmet was in they would not change it, and while one is finding the doctor one is very likely to get sunstroke.

May 7th – all demob has again been stopped as I hear there is trouble on the North West frontier. I am beginning to wonder if we shall ever get home. We are all absolutely fed up.

12 noon – I have just received orders to go with another wireless fellow to Risalpore on the frontier. We have been told nothing as regards our work there. We leave at 3pm today. Risalpore is 2000 miles away.

8pm – left Deolali at 3pm, well on our way now. Passed Nasvk some time ago.

May 9th – we are the first two wireless fellows called on for the frontier.

12:20 – we are near Jansi now. We had a fairly decent breakfast in the dining car. There are a lot of officers on this train who have been recalled to their regiments on the frontier.

2:30pm – Jansi stayed here a little while and had dinner, for which they charged R4 12. From papers etc we bought I see the Afghans have or are about to try to invade India, somewhere near the Khyber Pass.

4:15pm – Gwalior – had tea here. Gwalior fort is rather a fine looking place on a hill.

4:45pm – our train has just knocked down a native and killed him. Had late dinner on train. Reached Dheli late at night, stayed here nearly an hour.

May 10th – the dining car has been taken off so we shall have to wait until we get to a big station. Crossed the Sutlej River, it is very low now. Arrived Jullunder, but could not get anything to eat here.

1pm – Amritsar. This is where the chief trouble occurred. The station is well guarded by native troops.

3pm – Lahore, stayed here until 10:30pm. We had a good dinner at Monro's rooms. This is quite a nice place and very cheap.

10:30pm – left in an ambulance train which was going to Rawalpindi. We had spring beds etc, but it was impossible to sleep on them as the rocking of the train kept one jumping up and down.

When at Lahore I saw a lot of natives under escort, but everything seems to be quiet now. The native troops are with us, so nothing serious will happen. All officers are carrying rifles.

8am – Rawalpindi. We cannot get a train until 5:30pm so intend having a look around the place.

5pm – myself and Atkinson hired a gharry and had a drive around pindi, there isn't much of interest to be seen.

7:30pm – left for Nowshera, which is the end of our train journey.

12 midnight – Nowshera. We managed to wake the refreshment room people up and had some tea and bread and butter. We then laid our beds out on the platform and went to sleep.

May 11th - hired gharry and went to Risalpore, which we reached at 8:30am. We are for the present attached to 31st squadron RAF. There are about 20 of our craft from Meso here, Harrison and myself being the only two wireless operators.

The bungalows here are fairly decent but nothing to talk about. We are to start work on the squadron wireless here, listening in for Peshawar and Landi Kotal etc. Our aeroplanes, BE 2Cs, operate from here – they have been bombing the Afghans and have to fly over the mountains and tribal country before they get to Afghanistan. There is a landing ground at Landi Kotal, a fort on the Afghan side of the Khyber pass.

May 12th - Medical inspection at the hospital.

May 13th - Lt Barker and Hoare have come down in the tribes' country and have been captured. They will be lucky if they ever come out alive.

May 14th-17th - as usual I hear that the tribesman who captured Barker and Hoare will give them up on payment of the ransom. Each pilot who flies on this frontier carries a letter which states that a certain ransom will be paid to the tribe or tribesmen who brings the pilot safely into our lines. The Handley Page machine (small one)which arrived here today was overturned and smashed in a dust storm here this evening.

There appears to be a lot of sniping going on in the Khyber. We can hear Karachi sending from here. I heard them calling the Barpeta (the boat I went to Meso in) last night.

May 16th – the Afghans pretend they want peace, but it appears to be just to gain time to get round our fellows in Afghanistan.

May 17th - the fighting is increasing now. Some of the Khyber rifles have turned against us and are sniping our convoys going through the pass. We are losing a lot of men now.

May 18th - my birthday. I wonder how many more I shall spend in the army. Wrote letters. I haven't received a letter since March and I am anxious to hear that they are all right at home. We have a good view of the Himalayas from here. The snow on the top of the mountains was tinted pink by the rising sun this morning and they looked beautiful.

May 19th - the squadron are going to bomb Jalalabad tonight and tomorrow morning. I haven't heard anything from Deolali yet. Atkinson and myself had a tour around the place today but there is nothing of interest here. We are on the main road from Nowshera to Mardan. There are a lot of rocks on the Nowshera road - supposed to be marble, it certainly looks like marble. Before getting there one has to pass over the Kabul river, the railway and road cross it close to Nowshera.

The bazaar at Risalpore is very poor. There is a fairly decent

YMCA near here and also a native place where iced drinks etc are sold. There is also a supper bar, canteen and reading room.

May 20th – we have been put in orders as posted to this squadron. This is wrong, as we are only attached. We are going to see the OC.

May 21st – the Mohmands (tribes) have risen against us and there are rumours that they are coming this way. If anything like this happens we are to burn everything and retire to attack, which is the first line of defence in India.

May 22nd – our planes bombed a concentration of Mohmands at Shabkadr, but we haven't heard results yet. The big Handley Page arrived here from Lahore this morning, also a camel scout. The Handley Page is the one which flew out from Ipswich – it is going to bomb Kabul tomorrow. The pilot is a Captain Halley.

May 23rd – the Handley Page went over this morning and dropped bombs on Kabul on their way back. They passed Jalalabad, which they said was in flames owing to the bombing raid by our BE 2Cs this morning.

Received a long message from Shabkadar Fort about the Afghan council and impending attacks which we are to expect shortly.

All of us ex-Mesopotamian fellows went to the orderly room to see the adjutant about the conditions under which we came here. He said he had received a wing order to say that as soon as the Afghan trouble is over we shall be immediately released for demob. No matter where we are of course we don't put a great lot of trust in these promises.

It is getting hot here now, but we hope to have punkahs going in a few days.

May 25th - the pilot who took the Handley Page to Kabul said he dropped bombs on the Amir's Palace and on the Arsenal, but photos taken show the bombs bursting a good distance from the palace. He carried 9 x 112lb bombs and 20 x 20lb ones. The Afghans are again trying for an armistice but this is only to get going in another place. The best thing we can do is to wipe them out first and then talk about an armistice. The heads of affairs out here are as bad as a lot of women, they will talk for weeks but never do anything in the way of fighting. What India wants is a man with determination who says a thing and acts on it. I see in the Daily Mirror from England statements to the effect that we had volunteered to remain in India. I hear that all colonials out here are going or rather have gone home - they refused to remain out here and were backed up by their governments. Of course poor old English Tommy has to remain on and do the dirty work.

May 26th – some of our draft are going to Bannes tomorrow. Another draft of our fellows were coming here from Deolali but have been stopped owing to cholera there. Jalalabad according to photos taken from the air seems to have had rather a bad time about 1/3 of the city appears to have been burnt out. Lts Barker and Hoare have been released by the tribes. They were taken to Landi Kotal and are now back here not looking any the worse. They were very lucky in getting away alive. They were brought down in Bazaar Valley and captured. They could talk a little of the language so they could make them understand that they would get a ransom if they took them to Landi Kotal, which they did after a lot of arguments among themselves. B flight are going to Kohat tomorrow.

May 31st I have just received the order to proceed with 5 others to Peshawar, Harrison, Loades and Longbottom were with me. We asked the wireless officers Stewart and Mullinger what we were being sent away for, but they couldn't or more likely wouldn't tell us. I suppose we are bound for the frontier.

2:30pm left Risalpore by motor lorry reached Peshawar at 4pm. We went to Wing Headquarters. I understand I am to take charge of CRA station 1st Division who are at Landi Kotal at present so I am going further out that any of the rest. Longbottom is going within 10 miles of Landi Kotal to a fort called Ali Musijid – the others are remaining here. Landi Kotal is a fort on the Afghan side of the Khyber pass.

6pm – visited the soldiers home for tea etc and then had a stroll round the bazaars to purchase a few things. We stay here tonight and leave at 5am tomorrow morning. The officer in charge here (Stewart) is an absolute rotter. May he never see England again

June 1st, 5am – issued out with our stations. We use the same sort of tuner we had in Mesopotamia but all stations have 30ft iron masts I shall be all right as I am on headquarters with the General, but the fellows who are with mountain batteries will find it practically impossible to get them up into action. Two or three RE sections would be of much more use.

6:30am – we are on our way between Peshawar and Jamrud now. We were supposed to wait for the convoy at Peshawar but as it meant waiting about, we came on by ourselves. All of us had our rifles and revolvers loaded and ready.

7:30am Landi Kotal. The wind coming through the pass was terrific, it blew the hood off the car in places and at Ali Musjid, where we dropped Longbottom, the wind was so strong that when the tender stopped the car was forced backwards and we had to push behind to prevent it going over the Khud (cliff). We came up on the motor on the higher road, the lower road is for convoys etc. Between Ali Musjid and here the road is fairly good, it runs along the edge of a cliff for a long way and a wall of stones about 18" high is all there is to prevent a car going over if one skidded. The scenery is very wild with practically no vegetation to be seen or animals or birds.

6pm – I am at CRA now. they are in tents near the fort, the dust is awful here it blows under the tent and covers everything. I am at present in a 80lb tent with two of the CRA office fellows. We are moving into the fort tonight.

June 2nd – in the fort now. We have pitched our tent again as there isn't a building where we can stay in here. There are some decent bungalows here occupied by officers. This is the headquarters of the 1st Division. Gen. Fowler is in command and Gen. Bright (who I am with) is in charge of Divisional artillery. It is much hotter in here as we are surrounded by a high wall which prevents the wind getting in, it however keeps the dust out which is a good thing. The fort in peace time is garrisoned by native troops with white officers, but since this affair started, the Durhams have taken over.

The fort is situated in a hollow surrounded by hills, and there are several blockhouses on these hills which are in communication with the fort by helio and lamp. These blockhouses are built of bricks etc and are square with a flat roof. To get in a ladder is let down from the door, which is about 10 feet from the ground, and it is pulled after one.

There are several native villages near here. Each family appear to have a sort of fort to itself. They build a wall around the place and live in one corner of which in a tower which is a loopholed and in ordinary time when no British troops are here they carry on warfare between themselves. The watch tower is nearly always occupied by a fellow on the watch to snipe anyone he or the family has a grudge against.

June 5th – I go for a swim every night now at an open air bathing place about ½ a mile from the fort. There is one place for us and another for the Indian troops. It is about 5ft deep in places and the water is a dirty green - no doubt some thousands of fellows have washed in the same water, still it is this or nothing. There is a cemetery under the hills near here where some of the Ford Roberts troops were buried when he was fighting up here. The heat here is terrific. It is as much as we can stand and we only have a single cover tent so have to wear our helmets all the day in the tent. There is no canteen or YMCA here but we can expect nothing from muddling Indian authorities, they have muddled every frontier war they have undertaken as well as Mesopotamia.

The food isn't too bad here. All the staff here pay the native cook Rs5 per month to cook for us which he does very well, and one can sometimes get a few eggs from the natives. The staff captain asked me if I would like a horse, if so he would get me one, but as I should have to clean it and feed it etc I thought I would ride on the guns or on my A.T. cart which I have to carry my station when we move.

I have had four fellows from the batteries detailed to assist me in erecting my station and to use ground strips when working with aeroplane.

June 6th - they are getting large stores up here, which looks like a long stay here. Some EP tents have arrived - they are however I think being sent to Dakka. I hear there has been some scrapping at Thal.

June 7th - I had a rotten night last night with toothache, it nearly drove me silly and to makes things worse the sweat was pouring off me all the time.

June 8th - natives have started a little canteen here but the prices are awful, small cakes usually 6 annas each or R1.8 annas each. One can sometimes get a bottle of beer for which they charge R1.8 per bottle, which is equal to 3/6 in English money for a 1½ pint bottle. I however have no liking for beer.

There has been a shortage of water here during the last few days, owing I believe to the supply pipe breaking. The water is pumped here from the springs at Landi Khana (Bagh springs). we cannot get any water to drink and the water for our tea is taken from the reserve tank in the fort here.

The dust storms are awful here. Some of them last for 48 hours. I was out in one this evening and I couldn't see my hand before my face. It was practically impossible to breathe. No one seems anxious to start fighting again, I suppose it is too hot. In the fighting near here and at Bagh springs the Afghans had a good position but their artillery was useless. They had rather large guns which fired about one shell per minute and then the chances were it didn't go off. They had also some mountain guns but in the majority of cases the charge inside the shell would simply blow the nose cap off. Our artillery consist of 4.5 howitzers, 18 pounder, 3.5, and 2.7 mountain batteries. The 7th Brigade RFA M Battery RHA and no.6 Mountain Brigade are in this Division.

June 9th - dust very bad today. Mr Maritz (the Brigade Major) asked me if I would take charge of the liquors in the officers mess, but as I am a wireless operator and not a mess caterer I declined. I am not taking on any work of that sort. This little stunt is getting on my nerves. I understood when

I left Risalpore that I was urgently required here, but I haven't done anything yet and there is absolutely no sign of anything happening, besides we are doing the work of the 31st squadron operators who as soon as they heard that operators were wanted went sick. The temperature is well over 110 degrees in the shade and in the fort here under the tent it seems 200 degrees.

June 11th we get dust storms every day now, they usually come along about 7pm. We tie wet cloths over our mouths and nose to keep the dust out.

June 13th had some practice erecting stations etc with the fellows who are attached to me. There has I hear been some sniping at Nowshera. The drinking water is still very scarce, now and then we manage to get some out of the reserve. The YMCA has put up two EP tents here and sells cakes, tea, lime juice etc.

June 14th - wrote letters. One hears various rumours about going forward and also going back, we get situation and intelligence reports at headquarters here every day and I usually manage to see them. They are compiled from information received from spies and political agents who are in enemy country. This spy system is considered one of the best in the world. By this means we get to know what is happening at Kabul or Jalalabad and also when the tribes are preparing to raid us.

June 15th - two artillery fellows who have had a week's wireless course at Risalpore arrived today. One is to help me and the other is going to a mountain battery.

June 16th – the heat is very bad now. Hundreds of fellows have gone sick with heat stroke etc. Cholera is also very bad, especially at Ali Musjid. This country is about the worst I've ever seen and the conditions in this weather aren't fit for a white man to live under. It's no wonder a lot of fellows go mad.

June 17th – fellows are going sick in all directions here and cholera is very bad still, they have put a cholera camp not more than 500 yards from the fort.

June 18th rather cloudy today. We are absolutely praying for rain to keep this dust down and cool the air. There is an RE wireless set (VVK) in the fort here, they are in communication with Peshawar. I met Sgnt. Goff of the Durhams here today, he went out to Mesopotamia with us but got returned to his regiment. The 1st Sussex regiment are at Ali Musjid and the 1st Staffords at Landi Khana.

The mountain howitzers we are using are a new type of gun – this is the first time they have been used and they seem to be a great success. The Afghan soldier is armed with a rifle and bayonet some have the short Lee Enfield (same as our own), others have long Lee Enfields, while many are armed with rifles firing a lead bullet as big round as one's finger. If one of these hits one it makes a terrible wound. The tribesmen never take prisoners, or if they do it is only to torture them, anyone falling into their hands is subjected to awful mutilation before dying. It doesn't seem possible no doubt to people in England that such people exist, but to us out here it is a very real fact. It is of no use trying to correct these people by mean of missionaries, the only thing they recognise is force. Their motto is and always was "Might is right" and this is the deciding factor with them.

The Afghans are certainly more civilised than the tribes, but I shouldn't care to fall into their hands. The Amir appears to be under the influence of his Mullahs (chiefs), who are in most cases ignorant of the British resources.

The Afghan or the tribesmen are really no good as soldiers – they will wait behind a rock until our fellows are on them and then fire point blank. If they miss they will either Salaam a mark of respect or else run for it. Our fellows however never take prisoners unless forced to.

June 19th - I hear fighting is to start again on the 26th. In any case we are bound to win if the Indian Government keep awake. The Afridi rifles who used to guard the pass have been disarmed owing to a lot of them having deserted. They are called the Khyber rifles, as usually their duty in peace time is to guard the Khyber Pass against tribesmen. Their place has now been taken over by the Gurkhas, who are the finest fighters of the Indian army. One of our planes returning from Dakka today was shot at and hit nine times by tribesmen.

June 20th - some more of our fellows around here today from Peshawar, Simpson and Howlett are attached to 7th Brigade here. Colwell and File are going to Dakka and Reece to Landi Khana. They told me Harrison had gone sick at Peshawar and Lionel Hodges at Risalpur. It seems very likely that fighting will start again on the 26th as this is the end of Ramadan, the

Mohammedan feast. I have a 30ft iron mast still for my station, but all the others have had a 9ft pole substituted for their mast and being with the General do not take shoots when the Division are in action but check the other artillery stations.

June 21st – received letters from England, this is the first read since leaving Baghdad. I hear the Division is moving up to Dakka on Tuesday next. The 2nd Division are going to make headquarters here. I am not exactly keen on going to Dakka, from what I've heard it is a little hell. Still, one of two things will happen, I shall either pull through or go under. I'm beginning to think that if I stopped a shell in Mesopotamia it would have been the best way out. Still we must trust to luck and hope for the best.

June 22nd – have had toothache for the last two days, it is all along my jaw, it doesn't tend to make one happy. The heat here is terrible. It is worse than it was in Mesopotamia at 126 degrees in the shade.

June 23rd – the Afghans or tribesmen gave some of the Staffords a surprise today, when some of the staffs went up to picquet the hills this morning they found on reaching the top of one hill that the enemy had got up there during the night. They waited until our fellows were within a dozen yards and then fired on them, killing three and wounding several. One or two of the latter have since died, and they were buried in the cemetery here. The Divisional headquarters leave here tomorrow but I remain with the 7th Brigade RYA for a few days. The YMCA here is very slow, they have no games or decent books and the few papers about are American ones full of swank and praise for the American soldier. One paper had the sauce to say that the Americans smashed the German army and saved Paris and France. I wonder if it is possible to find a British paper whose articles praise up the English soldier like this. All the articles I've ever read in English papers are in praise of foreign or colonial troops. The hospital (field) is crowded with sick fellows.

June 24th - I am with Simpson at 7th Brigade now, the staff have gone to Dakka. We are outside the fort in an 80lb tent. I hear that the Germans have signed the treaty, this ought to have an effect on our friend the Amir.

June 25th - it is very hot here, we have to wear our spinepads and helmets all the day. I see that the Indian papers are advocating continuation of demob at once. There was a little sniping here last night. The nights here are fairly decent when there is no dust about, it is much cooler at night than it was in the fort. Our tent is situated between the horse and mule lines and natives sleep all round us, the natives usually develop a bad cough every night and this combined with restlessness of the horses etc and a few goats bleating gives one the impression of being in a farmyard.

June 27th - tribesmen were sniping us last night from the hills around. These are the Mohamands, one of the most powerful tribes on the frontier. Heard about the sinking of the German fleet.

This hot weather is awful from 7am until 6pm, one can only lie down in the tent and sweat. This gives one a washed-out feeling in the afternoon. One cannot keep one's boots on, they get so hot unless one is continually on the move.

June 29th 9:30am – a terrific dust storm blew up, it lasted an hour and we could hardly breathe and had to tie wet cloths over our mouths and noses.

12 noon – another dust storm. My eyes are full of dust, also my throat etc and we can barely speak or see. This is the day when the people in Blighty are celebrating peace. I wonder how many have thought of us out here.

12 midnight – another terrific dust storm followed by heavy rain which came under the tent and into my bed, which was of course on the ground. I was too fed up to move, I wouldn't have moved if it had rained ink.

June 30th – the dust has made my eyes rather bad, also my throat is very sore. I hope to heaven this affair will soon be over. A royal salute was fired today in honour of the signing of peace.

July 1st – going to Dakka tomorrow.

July 2nd, 6pm – we are at Sherabad now, a mile or two past Loe Dakka. We left Landi Kotal at 8:30am this morning.

The road from Landi Kotal to Landi Khana was along the edge of a cliff for a great part of the way and was a zig-zag road as it was downhill all the way. In places it was very steep, being as much as the horses and men could do to keep the guns back. We passed close to Bagh springs and the pumping station where the Afghans first started fighting. There are small blockhouses on many of the hills. We stayed at Landi Khana for water and fed for the horses. This place is some 2000ft below Landi Kotal, the camp here is right in the valley with high hills on every side. One could see tents on top of these hills showing where the picquets are. There was a good water supply there and the Staffs and some of the mountain artillery were there.

After leaving Landi Khana we met our escort of Sikh Lancers who came with us to Dakka. The country from Landi Kotal to just past Landi Khana is tribal country, after this comes Afghanistan. The country becomes much more flat now and also much hotter and one occasionally sees a tree or shrub now. The first Afghan fort or blockhouse is passed before one gets to the end of the pass, it is just a mud circular place about 30ft high and loopholed. There is a well just outside it.

A few miles further on we come to the end of the Khyber pass and the country opens out here, although there are hills on either side about 2 miles away. The heat along here was terrific and my skin was burnt to an amber colour. The road was very dusty but quite good enough for artillery.

Arrived at Sherabad after passing Loe Dakka at 3pm. We marched nearly all the way and were on the road in a temperature of well over 120 degrees in the shade for 7 hours. The horses were about done when we arrived, also ourselves.

July 3rd - couldn't sleep much last night, it was very hot. We are in a sort of compound or containment surrounded by a high mud wall. The CRA is outside about 300 yards away, I suppose I shall have to rejoin them. The dust is terrible here, it flows from morning till night. Some Afghan envoys arrived in our camp this evening with a white flag.

July 4th – we were sniped last night by enemy over the other side of the river (Kabul) but they only killed one Indian. Our fellows replied with machine guns and a mountain gun. The camp here is right in the hills, we have picquets on most of these hills. Lalpura is just across the river. The Kabul river is rather nice to bathe in in the evenings, although the current is rather strong. The tribesmen get over the other side of the river and snipe at us while we are bathing, but they have to be good shots to hit any of us. Three machine gun sections are told off to reply to these fellows when they start shooting.

A scrap took place here this afternoon. Some of the enemy tried to get our picquets. Our batteries opened on them and the Dragoons went through the Chota Khyber pass to cut them off, they however retired.

July 5th – there was a lot of firing during the night and it is still going on. One of our mountain batteries has gone to support our cavalry – we are supporting them with 4.5 howitzers and 18 pounders.

Later – the enemy have retired again, they got more than they wanted.

July 6th – received orders to return to the General. Three other fellows are going with me to help me. I hear we are going on to Jalalabad. The tribesmen (Mohmands) tried to get our picquets again but we opened fire on them I killed about 100 of them, they then retired.

6pm - went over to CRA. The dust is two feet deep about here and when the wind blows it is terrific.

July 7th - the camp was sniped last night from over the river and also from the hills behind us. They evidently have the headquarters here ranged, as most of the bullets hit near us or go just over. A fellow was knocked out by an elephant bullet in the tent next to ours. I was sleeping outside as it was too hot in the tent, but after one or two elephant bullets came within a few yards of me I thought it was time to get inside. We have dug down about two feet inside the tent so as to have some protection. A dust storm blew up during the night and we could barely speak in the morning.

July 8th - I slept out last night and fixed up a sort of barricade of stones and my small tent rolled up. Just as I was going to get my bed down at 9:30pm some tribesmen let off a volley into the camp, and soon afterwards our fellows started firing mountain guns and machine guns. I wonder how many people in England know there is a war on out here?

July 9th - very hot today, there seem to be a lot of tribesmen about in the hills as they are continually firing at us. We killed about fifty of them yesterday towards the Jalalabad plain near a place called Girdi. We were fired at while bathing this evening but no one was hit. Later on the Gurkhas brought in 9 tribesmen who were armed with Martini rifles - one had a sort of 12-bore sporting gun. The 38th battery RFA has just arrived from Peshawar - they say there are a lot of troops there now. I have a small telescope here and with it I can see the people walking about in Lalpura over the river. It is built very much like an Arab town and made chiefly of mud. There is a sort of compound surrounded by high walls about 200 yards away from it, I believe this is where the snipers get at nights.

July 10th - our machine guns were going nearly all the night.

July 11th - sniping again from 5pm to 7:30pm - a few Indians were hit close to our tent. Received letters.

July 12th - a lot of the enemy got on top of a hill overlooking the camp and fired at us. Our machine guns started, also mountain guns and 4.5 howitzers. Some of the tribesmen would wave then shout at us, also fire their rifles. They don't appear to be afraid of shells but when one goes off they pick up the pieces. One of the 4th battery was shot by snipers last night.

July 13th - a dust storm has been blowing for nearly 24 hours and we have simply breathed dust during this time. Heaven knows what our lungs are like.

July 14th - thank heaven the dust storm is over, it finished about 3am this morning and was followed by a good shower of rain.

7pm - two or three tribesmen are at present on the top of the hill behind Alpura waving a shirt or something. They dodge down as soon as they hear our guns go off. They will stop a shell or bullet one of these days if they get too saucy.

July 15th - some of the enemy got through our picquet last night and fired into the camp, the picquets caught one when he was trying to get back. The dust is awful today.

July 16th - plenty of dust blowing about. Mr Stewart from the wing visited me today. I asked him about demob, but he couldn't tell me anything.

July 17th - the snipers livened us up last night. The nullters were humming all round me. I soon made tracks for the tent until things had got a bit quiet as I had no wish to stop an elephant bullet. It's about time our people started clearing these tribes out of the hills - if I had my way I would blow Lalpura to bits if the sniping didn't stop.

One gun which one of the snipers use makes a louder noise than the others and the bullet he fires makes a noise like a small shell going through the air. We call this fellow "Charlie", and whenever someone hears his rifle they say "hullo, Charlie is on again tonight". He is quite an old pal of ours now. If he gets killed we shall miss his nightly entertainment.

July 18th - I had a near shave last night. I was out near our native cookhouse (tent) and another fellow was talking and had his hand on the tent pole when an elephant bullet passed by between his body and the pole, going through the tent at the back. A sniper got through our picquet and shot two of the 4th battery horses. An elephant bullet fired from over the river came through the officers' mess, tent hitting the table between two fellows, and then came through our tent in the wall.

July 19th – we had a storm of rain last night, which did a lot of good in laying the dust. The Afridis near Ali Musjid have captured one of our posts and are holding up the pass. Our convoys cannot get through, so our supplies are for the present cut off.

July 20th – the snipers sent over a few volleys last night. They all seem to direct their fire on the headquarters, here I suppose they know where the General is.

Our General (Fowler) here seems afraid to use ammunition. The other day we had information that a number of the enemy were in some trees about two miles away, but he wouldn't let the artillery fire on them as he didn't want to use up ammunition. I don't expect he has ever been in a decent scrap to know what using ammunition means.

July 21st – two Afghan messengers came into our lines today. Our people at Ali Musjid have driven the Afridis back, but the pass is still closed for convoys.

July 22nd – two Afghan delegates came into camp today and I understand a big Afghan delegation is coming through on the 24th to arrange peace at Rawalpindi. It's about time something happened, we are all absolutely fed up with this stunt.

July 23rd – Charlie was shooting again last night. The weather is very hot and the sweat pours out of one from morning till night. The tribesmen to the number of about 8000 made an attack on our position here today – they captured one of our posts and killed about 12 of our fellows, including one officer.

The Yorks and Gurkhas under cover of our guns soon had them out of it again. When our fellows recaptured the hill they found that the tribesmen had started skinning our officer and mutilated one or two other fellows.

These tribesmen are absolute fiends. Every white man the capture they mutilate terribly before killing them. The women are just as bad as the men. We read articles in English papers about bombing Kabul and killing innocent women and children. Let the people who write these articles come out here and see some of our boys after these devils have finished with them.

The Afghans offered a sum of 7 lacks of rupees to the tribe who turned us out of Dakka, and I suppose the attack today was by the Mohmand tribe after the money. The tribe who turns us out of here will earn this money. The Afghans arrive tomorrow.

July 24th – the Afghan delegation arrived in our lines this morning at 10:45am. The chief delegates rode in two Daimler motor cars – they had a large number of followers. In the front car was the commander in chief of the Afghan army, who wore a large black plume in his hat. Most of the chief delegates were old men with white beards. They were all armed with rifles, revolvers, swords etc. The rifles they had were the same as we use (short Lee Enfield). No honours were paid them in any form – we felt more like shooting them.

All our artillery infantry etc had received orders to be on parade and some to go down the road towards Landi Khandi and to meet the delegation to make out that they were fresh troops just arriving. Some of the infantry met the Afghans at one end of the camp then went back and met them again at the other end. It was all a game of bluff to make the delegation think we had more men than we really have.

The tribesmen stopped the Afghans near Girdi and had a long talk with them - we do not know what it was about, but our spies will no doubt find out. The driver of one of the Afghans cars could speak English. He said the arsenal was not destroyed by our Handley Page when it went over Kabul.

July 25th - read letter. Charlie sent over a few rounds last night. I see the Indian government in reply to questions in various papers have published an answer in regard to conditions and feeding of troops on the frontier. It looks very well on paper but is rather different in reality.

July 26th – the commander in chief of the Indian army (Gen Monro) visited our camp this morning. It was very nice this morning, no dust about. He went back after staying an hour or so, I wish he had stayed as a dust storm blew up this afternoon.

"Simy" (wireless op at 7th Brigade) has been put under open arrest for refusing to help lay a telephone line. The signal officer threatened to shoot him. I told him to cheer up as it would prevent him from dying of cholera.

July 27th - a few tribesmen tried to get into camp last night (they got in a few nights ago and stole some camels) but some

Gurkhas were out waiting for them and caught some of them. Early this morning I saw some of them coming into camp carrying the heads of the tribesmen under their arms. They put one of these heads on a pole outside their lines and stuck a cigarette into its mouth.

July 28th – an order has come to the Division that all Mesopotamian men are to be sent to Deolali for concentration previous to being sent home. The CRA has wired to wing to ask them to recall them. The wing has wired to say that they have no reliefs for us at present so cannot recall us. I should like to strangle the people who are responsible for this fooling.

July 29th – all the Meso fellows in the infantry and artillery have had orders to return to Deolali. I wonder if the RAF will play any tricks on us.

Grant at Pindi peace conference told the Afghan delegates what to expect if they don't accept our terms. The Afghan CIC in reply said that Britain had made the first move towards ending the war and that England had only won the great war by combining with other powers, and he hinted that Afghanistan could do the same.

Two or three Afghan messengers have gone through today on their way to consult with the Amir about some question at the conference. The Afghan delegates at Pindi said they were surprised that our fellows didn't salute them as they entered our lines at Dakka, as if they were going to salute a dirty lot of niggers.

July 30th – all the Meso men with the exception of 4 of us RAF and a few Sigs have gone back to Deolali. The RAF haven't applied for us yet – we appear to be going to be left again. However if we do not get recalled soon we shall see the General and put our case before him.

July 31st – wrote to Atkinson to hear what the fellows at Risalpur are doing about demob. There has been practically no sniping since the Afghans went through. This is chiefly owing to some of our Gurkhas being over the river at nights now waiting for them.

Aug 1st – we have had an awful dust storm all day. I have swallowed enough to start a garden.

Aug 2nd – we haven't heard anything definite about what is going on at the peace conference at Pindi, but things do not appear to be going very easily.

August 3rd – there is nothing happening here now. We hear plenty of rumours, some about going forward and back to Landi Kotal. The peace conference is being held in camera, so there is no official news published. The weather is very changeable now, one day being very close and hot, the next being very windy and cold.

Our force here consists of the 1st Indian Division, which has about three white regiments in it, the rest being Indians and Gurkhas. There are no Mohammedan regiments owing to the fact that the Afghans and tribes are Mohammedans. The Gurkha is the best fighting man, with Sikh next, in the Indian army.

Aug 4th – Simpson and myself saw Capt Shears about demob and leave, but all he could tell us was that as soon as peace was signed at Pindi or any reliefs arrive we should be recalled. He said there were no other wireless fellows in India who could take our place.

Aug 5th – I bought a few Afghan coins here at the Bazaar today. I tried to get a curious looking one, but the fellow wouldn't sell it. Nearly all the articles sold in this bazaar come from India.

Aug 6th – Howlett, who went to Peshawar, is now in Pindi hospital with malaria and debility.

Aug 7th – the Afghan messengers who came through our lines to return to Kabul have returned. They have gone on to Pindi. It was very dusty last night. I tried to sleep outside but could not stand it, so I had to retire to the tent.

Aug 8th – had a thunderstorm last night. I was sleeping outside the tent and the rain woke me up before I had got very wet. I have got leave to go to Murree for 7 days – I go with a party of fellows tomorrow

2:30pm – just heard that peace has been signed with Afghanistan at Rawalpindi at 11 am this morning. So another war is over. I wonder how many more I shall see before getting home.

I haven't mentioned our sleep walker before, but we have a fellow in our tent who walks, or rather runs, in his sleep. The second night after he arrived he crawled over us and rushed out of the tent yelling at the top of his voice. He ran through our horse lines, fell in a big hole, got out of that and then ran another 200 yards before he woke up. If he had run another 100 yards he would have run into a Gurkha sentry who would no doubt have taken him for a tribesman and brought him down. Since this we always tie him to the tent pole at nights. Several times he has got up and tried to bolt but the rope pulls him up.

Aug 9th – every morning we make a recce towards a village called Girdi to see what the enemy are up to. This little affair is as good as a play – the following usually happens. Just to the west of Sherabad is a ridge of hills through which runs a pass called the Khurd or Chola Khyber. On either side of this pass is a hill occupied night and day by our picquets, they go by the names of Emergency Picquet and Black Hill. The other side of this ridge is a small plain and then comes another ridge with another pass which leads out on to the plains of Jalalabad near Girdi. This ridge is occupied by our fellows every morning – we have two picquets here called West Spur and Conical Hill. Just past this ridge is a hill called Camel Back which is just out of range of our guns firing from the camp.

Every morning our troops have to occupy West Spur and Conical Hill. They stay here for a time and then retire. The cavalry go through the Khurd Kyber Pass and also machine gun sections and take up a covering position. The infantry then go up and occupy the picquets, staying there long enough to find out where the enemy are and then retire, leaving a rear guard to cover the retirement. In the meantime the tribesmen, knowing what time our fellows occupy these picquets, get up on the top of Camel Back hill (Which we call the Grandstand and sit down or stand about and watch our people occupy the two picquets). When our fellows retire they stroll down the hill smoking and talking with their rifles slung on their back and then some of them pass through Girdi while others cross the road and come up the hills to the picquet shelter which our fellows have just vacated. They climb to the top and then start firing at our fellows retiring. Our machine guns and sometimes artillery reply to this. When they get tired of shooting or our fellows get out of range, they sit down and smoke etc. After this they collect all the bullets, bits of shell, cartridge cases etc they can find and retire.

This little game occurs every morning. The other morning however, the tribes occupied the picquet positions before our fellows got there and hid behind rocks. They waited until our fellows got within a few yards and then opened fire, killing several of the Yorks and Gurkhas. It took artillery fire and three attacks by infantry to turn them out.

Aug 9th – left Dakka at 6:15am this morning in Ford cars and arrived at Landi Khana at about 7am. The fellows at Haft Chah Post have made 'heatstroke station' in letters of white stone on the ground outside. This post was originally the first Afghan outpost. Met Lees at Landi Khana.

10am – left in AT carts for Landi Kotal. This is the worst portion of the pass, being uphill all the way. The road is cut out of the cliff and just wide enough for two mule carts to pass. Our people are evidently going to retain Bagh Springs and the pumping station as there are hundreds of Indians working there and also improving the road from Landi Kotal.

Arrived at Landi Kotal about 8am. It has altered a lot since I was here last. Most of the white troops appear to have gone. We are staying in the rest camp here tonight and go through to Jamrud Fort tomorrow. The evenings are rather cold here now.

Aug 10th, 8pm – I am now at Jamrud rest camp. We left Landi Kotal at 6:15am this morning in motor lorries and arrived here at about 8:30am. We came along the top road.

Ali Musjid has altered a great deal, the camp being about 4 times as large as it was when I was here in June. There is a battery of 6" guns there now. It is hotter here than it was at Landi Kotal, but there is a decent YMCA in the fort where one can get a nice drink or a meal.

Aug 11th - the Viceroy has just passed through (8am). He is going to Dakka I believe, I hope there is a nice dust storm waiting for him there. I tried to get permission to go into Peshawar to get my overcoat, but the officer in charge is afraid to let anyone leave the party, so I shall have to do without one at the moment.

6pm - left by train for Rawalpindi, we got into second class carriages and were settled down when we were told these carriages were for sergeants etc and we had to carry all our kit to the other end of the train and get into filthy third class native carriages.

Aug 12th, 6:30am – Rawalpindi, we went to the hospital for breakfast where I saw "Abdul" Sparrow, Mathews and a fellow who used to be the Colonel of 222 Brigade's orderly. He said that Bogey Campbell has died at Deolali. I was very sorry to hear that Bogey was one of the lost.

8am – moved off in motor lorries to the hills – the road for about 20 miles isn't very steep. We stayed at Tret for about 20 minutes to have some tea etc. The scenery from here becomes much finer and the road winds round and round and is fairly steep.

As we get near Sunny Bank one has a fine view of various other stations on hills in the distance, some of which are partly hidden by clouds, which owing to the monsoon weather are hanging low now. At Sunny Bank some of the fellows branched off to Barian, but I went on to Murree and went to the leave camp, which is on the football ground not far from the skating rink. This place is 7000ft above Rawalpindi.

August 13th – I met Vic Jesses here last night. He is on 7 days' leave, the same as myself, but he goes back today . He is staying at Lower Topa. He said Lionel Hodges and several other RAF fellows were down there.

Visited the cinema last night to see the picture "Lest We Forget". There were a good few English women there but what objects they were. It would be impossible to find a worse-looking lot in Blighty. Thank heaven there are some different women in England.

The weather here is very damp - it rains every day. The air also is very damp and the mist and clouds which come into our tents make our blankets quite wet.

Aug 14th - visited pictures to see "Derelicts" and Jimmy Wilde v. Lynch fight, the pictures shown here are very good. We had a little sunshine today with occasional showers, what a difference this is to Dakka.

Aug 15th - bought camera for Rs30.8 so I hope to take some snaps now. Had a walk to upper Lopa and had dinner at the soldiers' home, where I met P Ness. I then went down to Lower Lopa and saw L Hodges, Atkinson, Young and several other of our draft who are up on leave.

Went to see Humphrey Bishop's company at the theatre last night but I didn't think a great deal of them. They charged rather stiff prices - about ¾ of the hall comprised Rs5 seats or one could get a back seat for R3.

Aug 16th - visited the theatre last night to see "The Futurists" (74th Battery party). It was a much better show than Humphrey Bishop's and it was also free to soldiers, which no doubt accounted for a full house. There was an Indian army order out that all ex-Meso men evacuated from hospital were to be sent to Deolali for demob, but the RAF people say it doesn't apply to us, we have to go back to our units if we go to hospital. Several of our fellows went sick to get away like this, if they haven't already got away they will be unlucky.

Received a telegram from Risalpur to tell me to report there on termination of leave instead of going back to Afghanistan.

Aug 17th – went on the rink today. This is our last day here – we go down tomorrow. It is still very wet here with rain every day. The country about here is very similar to the Simla Hills and all the hills are covered with a kind of pine tree, which look very nice. There are several stations in these hills, the chief of which is Murree, which is on the main Kashmir road. There are some rather decent shops in the mall here and "Belgie" has a shop there. There are a lot of civilians about who come up here from Pindi, Peshawar etc during the hot weather.

Aug 18th – visited the pictures last night. Leaving here at about 1:30pm today. There are some glorious views from here when the weather is fine. Am at Pindi now. We had a very wet journey down from Murree, it rained in torrents for hours before we started and we had to go to where the lorries were waiting for us in the rain. The consequence was that all fellows who had no overcoat or caps were wet through and had to remain like that until they got here. I was rather fortunate as I could make my waterproof ground sheet into a cape, so I managed to keep fairly dry.

We had only gone about three miles when we were forced to stop, owing to the road in places being nothing but a raging torrent. Great stones and rocks had been washed down the hills and blocked the road, while the water was pouring across the road waist deep. However, after a time the rain stopped and then natives started clearing the road of rocks, so eventually we got through.

Aug 19th – arrived at Nowshera last night and slept on the platform. Some lorries came down to meet us this morning and brought us here (Risalpore). I understand we are going on a draft next Wednesday.

August 20th – Simpson, Colwell and the other operators who were on the frontier and Afghanistan are back here now.

Aug 21st – we are still waiting for news about demob.

Aug 22nd our draft has been cancelled by the Simla people. They state that we shall not be relieved until men can be brought out from England to replace us. If they start those little games I can see trouble in the near future. We are not on parades here, there is no earthly reason for our detention and we aren't going to stand any more fooling.

Aug 23rd – the General is inspecting the squadron on Tuesday and all of us Mesopotamian fellows are putting in an application to see him. We are getting desperate now. If we do not get satisfaction from the General we intend to cable the Air Ministry or the Labour leader in England.

Aug 25th – we have seen Carberry again. He tried to bluster and say he would keep us as long as he wanted, but I think he is afraid about seeing the General.

Aug 26th – I hear that we are leaving here tomorrow. Carberry evidently wants to get rid of us before the General comes.

Aug 27th – have been paid Rs200 and had our demob papers checked, so no doubt we are going at last. 5pm – left in lorries for Nowshera.

Aug 31st, 8am – arrived at Deolali. The journey down was uneventful, but the monsoon season is here now and the country this side of Lahore was flooded in places and rivers are in flood. Official figures state that out of 100,000 troops in the Afghan war there were 50,000 hospital cases, chiefly fever and heatstroke. This gives one an idea of the conditions prevailing there.

Sept 1st – we parade every morning here for roll call, but we do no other parades. We are in no 6 camp. Met Parnell at the YMCA last night, also "Bob" who was with our Brigade in Meso.

Sept 2nd – it rains every day now. It is miserable in these tents and there is nowhere to go with the exception of the YMCA Deolali, which is about 2 miles away. One has to get there 1 1/2 hours before the show starts and line up to get a seat.

Sept 3rd-10th – moved into no. 5 camp. The food is very poor here, someone is making a fortune out of it.

Sept 11th – a draft has been called out to sail next Monday from Bombay. I hope to get on the next.

Sept 12th – I have been put on a draft which sails from Bombay on the Stephan on the 16th. Have been paid Rs120.

Sept 13th – paraded for CO's inspection. I am writing home by this mail but with luck I should be there as soon as the mail.

Sept 14th – we leave tomorrow, if all goes well.

Sept 15th – left camp at 7:30pm and arrived at the station to find that owing to a mistake there were not enough coaches on the train to take all of us, so we had to wait until 1am before we could get away. (Sept 16th) But these are the little trials one must get used to in India, it would have surprised us much more if the train had started to time, such an occurrence is unknown out here.

We arrived at Bombay all right and went straight off the train to the boat after having a strict medical inspection, each man being given a ticket without which one could not go on the ship.

5pm – am now at sea on the SS Stephan, a Booth Line boat of 4500 tons. We left Alexandria docks about 1:20pm. A native band played for an hour or so on the quay before we left, but we didn't want them. When they played the National Anthem the fellows simply made cat calls and laughed – it shows what feelings the Government has put into fellows by their treatment of men who were more patriotic than the majority in 1914. We have been caught once, but never again.

Now that I have left India I will try and sum up the country conditions etc there as briefly as possible.

Conditions in India

The civilians (white) have a fairly decent time there, having natives to do everything for them and having every convenience such as electric fans, nice airy bungalows etc for their comfort. As there are not many white families in the small towns they all know each other and visit each other, one being as it were on the same level.

The white women do practically no work and usually only come out in the evenings when it is cool. In some parts of India the white women and children go to the hills during the hot weather on the plains. There are hill stations in South, Central and North India. These stations have a climate very similar to England.

The white children seem to be educated far beyond their years as little boys of about 8 years will talk to one like a grown-up person. The women treat the lower-class natives as they do animals and they also look down on the British Tommy - they never get up concerts or socials for the troops. If however the natives rise or there is going to be trouble, some of these women will come round to the YMCA etc and sing to the troops just to make out that they want to amuse the fellows. In ordinary times they wouldn't come near one. I think the chief reason is that they were so used to treating a soldier as something beneath them for so many years in peace time that they cannot get out of the habit.

At Bangalore we were not allowed into the club or library. I suppose they thought we should start destroying the books like a lot of savages, but there are a great number of our fellows who are better educated and come from better homes than it is possible to find in Bangalore. The natives chiefly down the south are fairly loyal but the natives in the north, who are Muhammedans, would rise whenever they thought they would be successful. The majority of natives are only kept in subjection by the presence of our troops out here. I wouldn't give much for the chances of the white civilians if we were withdrawn.

The natives in the villages and towns seem to do exactly as they like. They manage their own affairs although a white fellow usually superintends the various districts – he is called the Commissioner. He is directly over the native police of his district. In some of the large cities of the north it is not safe for white fellows to enter unless in a number and during the day. Most of these cities have a British garrison who live at the forts in case of riots etc. The white civilians take refuge in these forts, which are capable of holding several thousand persons.

The natives in the villages live like animals. Filthy dogs, pigs, cows etc go into the huts where the people live when they like. The people have no idea of sanitation, nor do they seem to want any improvements. This state of affairs is the main cause of plague, cholera and other diseases which rage out here.

Each village has a god of its town, usually a stone painted with a kind of red and decorated with flowers. When disease breaks out in a village the people hold a festival to please the god. These festivals are very weird and usually include animal sacrifices and sprinkling their blood around the village to keep the evil spirits away. Sometimes I have heard these natives beating tum-tums (drums) all night to drive the evil spirits away.

Sept 17th – well out now. We are packed like herrings and it is impossible for half of us to sleep below. I slept on deck last night and that was crowded – still, it is better than sleeping in the awful atmosphere down below. The decks during the day are crowded and if one wants a place he has to get there first and stay there or he will have no place to sleep at night.

Sept 23rd - hope to sight land tomorrow at the entrance to the Red Sea. The journey up to the present has been a very bad one. The conditions under which we are travelling are not fit for white men. I understand there are about 60 men ill already. I don't know what things will be like in the Red Sea.

I saw a whale yesterday, about ½ mile away. Up to the present we have travelled about 1300 miles.

Sept 23rd - we reach Aden tomorrow morning. The sea is rather better today but during the last few days there has been a rotten swell which made it very unpleasant.

The evenings are rather nice now on deck, owing to the breeze which comes up. It is however very hot below. We pass thousands of jellyfish which float just below the surface of the water. They are rather pretty, being composed of a pink centre with light green or blue surrounding it. There are also hundreds of dolphins which jump clear of the water and turn a somersault in the air.

Sept 24th - Passed Aden, we hope to reach Perim this afternoon. I shouldn't like to be stationed here. There are only a few bungalows here and a signal station on a hill, the surrounding country is very barren.

7pm – just passed a battleship and also a passenger boat , the passengers waved to us.

Later – passed a ship which called us up by lamp, I read what she had to say, she said she was the City of Chester. They were bound from Malabar Coast to Marseilles and Liverpool and asked us how many troops we had on board.

It is getting warm in the evenings now, the sun sets on our flank now so it is too hot to stay on the port side of the boat after about 4pm as the sum beats in so. If we had about half the number of troops on board it wouldn't be so bad, but the starboard side of the ship won't hold all of us. We are 1970 miles out from India now and it is 970 miles to Suez.

Some of our fellows have I hear gone down to help stoke the ship, as several of the stations have gone owing to the heat.

Sept 25th – the heat is terrific, I have a bad headache and cold. It is a little hell on this boat now, but we would stand anything to get home.

I will give an average day's routine:

6am – turn out as the deckhands wash down the decks. There is a terrific taste in one's mouth on waking owing to the close atmosphere. We stay on deck until 7:30 when we go below for breakfast. As soon as we get there we start sweating, and by the time breakfast is over shirts are wet through. As soon as breakfast is done we rush up on deck and find a spare place to sit down. The air is fairly cool about this time on deck.

At 11am we get boat stations and then we sit on deck crowded as niggers until 1pm, when we go below for dinner, which is a repetition of breakfast only several degrees hotter. Most of the fellows take all their clothes off except a pair of shorts when down below. After dinner we go on deck again and lie down until about 3:30pm, when the sun comes round and make the deck too hot for us, so we go in search of a shady place until tea time, which is at 5pm. We then have another sweat bath during tea, after which we get once more on deck until the next morning. We spend hours at night looking out to sea and wondering if it is really possible that we are going home.

Sept 26th - I saw a shark near the ship today.

Sept 27th - still very hot. We hope to reach Suez tomorrow. Inspection for plague by the doctor.

Sept 28th - arrived at Suez about 8:30am and remained here for two or three hours. Two fellows who were ill have been left in Suez hospital. There is an Italian boat and a Dutch liner near here, also an American cruiser.

2pm - moving up the canal. The canal banks seem deserted now, it is rather different to when we passed here nearly 4 years ago. A searchlight has been fitted to our ship so I suppose we shall keep on the move all through the night. We passed a sunken Italian battleship at Suez.

11pm - our boat has to put into the side sometimes to let other ships pass - some of them have troops on board just going out. Our fellows shouted out and told them they were five years too late.

Sept 29th – a rather amusing incident happened last night. We have brought with us from Suez a native boat and two natives to make the ropes fast to the bank whenever we want to stop. About midnight last night our boat wanted to put in to the side and let another boat pass, so our people let down the natives into their boat, which was beneath the anchor, and after a few minutes, thinking the natives had got away, they dropped the anchor. The boat however had not gone, so the anchor went through it like through a piece of paper, filling it with water and throwing the two natives out. A boat was launched from the ship and a lifebelt was thrown over our boat. We picked up one fellow and took their boat in tow while an Egyptian boat picked up the other fellow. They tried to pull the native boat out of the water, but it broke to pieces, so it was left in the canal, the two natives being taken on board.

Sept 29th – arrived Port Said this morning and anchored just outside the port. There is a big Armenian refugee camp near here, they are chiefly in tents but there are a lot of decent wooden buildings. We are taking in coal and frozen meat etc. A big ship carrying troops has just passed us going outwards – a lot of chaff passed between us.

7pm – going out now, our fellows are singing songs on deck. Thank heaven we are at last out of the East.

Sept 30th - well out now in the Mediterranean. The sea is rather nice.

Oct 1st - the sea was rather choppy last night and the portholes were closed to prevent the water coming in. There is an order out that all men are to sleep below in future owing to the change in the climate, but it is impossible for all of us to sleep below. The people at Bombay in charge of embarkation evidently take us for cattle, not men. However we shall refuse to go below, we would rather take our chance and sleep on deck, as it is very much better than sleeping like pigs below.

It is cold enough for serge clothing in the evening now. At noon today we were 410 miles out from Port Said and 520 from Malta.

Oct 2nd - we get absolutely no exercise on this boat. There is no room to walk about as the decks are always packed with fellows lying on the floor and it takes one about 10 minutes to pick one's way from end to end of the ship. The fellows on board play crown and anchor a lot and I saw a fellow lose about £200 in less than 10 minutes the other night. I should be surprised if the banker doesn't win over £1000 before he gets to England.

Oct 3rd, 2pm - passed Malta and Gozo. I took a snap of Valetta. We passed a waterspout on the port side this afternoon - it was a very large one and stretched from the clouds in a kettle spout shape to the sea. The sea below us was disturbed, giving off a cloud of spray. After a while the waterspout gradually grew shorter until it disappeared into the clouds again. The weather is nice now and I still sleep on deck. It is all right if one puts plenty of clothes over one.

Oct 4th – passed some islands, evidently off the coast of Tunis. We hope to reach England in a week's time.

Oct 5th – we can see the Algerian coast now, it is very hilly. The sea has been rather choppy today and the ship is rolling and dipping a good deal.

Oct 6th – the sea is still choppy and a strong headwind is blowing. We only did 228 miles during the last 24 hours. Passed a destroyer, no. 133, at noon today. It is getting quite chilly at nights now and I usually put a blanket and two coats over myself.

7:30pm – passed a ship which sent us a message by lamp. She said that the railwaymen and transport workers' strike had been settled in England, and she gave her name at the Maresfield, bound from Columbo to Rotterdam.

Oct 7th – Gibraltar. We didn't stay here, only went in close to the rock. It is very strongly fortified, some naval guns being on the top of one of the high rocks. The side of the rock looking east has great concrete beds let into the side of the hill – this is I believe to collect water. There is a sort of overhead trolley which runs from the bottom to the top of the hill, evidently used to convey stores etc. to the top. The harbour is on the west side and there were a lot of cargo boats there today. The barracks, wireless station etc are situated chiefly on the southern side, but there appears to be a town near where the Spanish territory joins the rock.

5pm - going through the Straits fairly close to the Spanish coast. The country is very hilly and there are solitary houses in these hills built of white stone or painted white with red tiled roofs. I should imagine it is very lonely living there. We passed a lot of dolphins jumping about in the water.

Oct 8th - the sea was rather choppy last night but is fairly calm now. I am heartily fed up with this journey. It has been more or less a nightmare to me.

10am - passing Cape St Vincent. We are quite close in. The lighthouse on the headland is rather a large one of white material. I took two snaps here, but the light wasn't very good. The country (Portugal) about here is very barren and houses are scattered at wide intervals. The land rises directly out of the sea for about 100ft. These cliffs have numerous caves caused by the action of the water.

6pm - passing Cape Espichel about 30 miles south of Lisbon. We can see another headland in the distance, presumably Cape da Roca.

7:30pm - passing mouth of the Tagus river. There are several lighthouses or lightships near the entrance and one light revolves alternately white and red.

Passed Cape da Roca - it has a big lighthouse. Our boat has a roll on now.

Oct 9th – there was a beautiful sunrise this morning. About five minutes before the sun rose in the east the moon went down in the west, it was a bright red and looked like the sun rising. We hope to reach Cape Finisterre at the beginning of the Bay of Biscay tonight. We are wearing serge clothing now, but I still sleep on deck and I mean to remain there until we get to England.

Oct 10th – we are in the bay now. We passed Cape Finisterre, so she may catch us up.

Oct 11th – well out in the bay now. There is a strong sea running and also a very cold NE wind blowing which goes through one.

Oct 12th – hope to reach Devonport tonight. 8pm – passed Ushant off the French coast. I believe we reach England about 4am tomorrow morning. The sea is calmer now, but the wind is very cold. We are in the Channel now. No one appears to be excited. They have all waited so long for this time but the way we have been treated takes all the gilt away.

Oct 13th – arrived in Plymouth Sound at 2am. It is very cold here. We have now moved up to just outside Devonport and it is very foggy, it looks as if they could do with a bit of sun here. The other ship arrived about the same time as ourselves.

Oct 14th – we have been waiting on deck for three hours in a cold wind waiting for a tug to take us ashore. We are getting fed up with this waiting about. 2pm – on shore at last. We saw some civil workers for the first time and we saw a policeman on the quay - he looked very funny in his uniform after getting used to native police. We gave him a good cheer, which quite startled him. A band played on the quay when we landed, but there were no people about to see us come in. we expected a better welcome than this, but I suppose all the welcomes have been used up on the Colonials and Americans.

After being issued with a train ration at the YMCA I sent a wire home. We then boarded the train and went via Exeter and Yeovil to Fovant, not far from Salisbury, to be demobilised.

Oct 15th - left for home via Salisbury, arrived home about 7:30pm.

In journeys alone I travelled approximately twenty four thousand miles (24,000) during my period abroad.

Oswald S. Early

Some of the wireless stations I used to read when in Mesopotamia (Call position and nature of work)

DAS – DAMASCUS - A very powerful note station, he works a lot with Constantinople and MED (Medina). He used to work with MED night and day. One of his tricks is to send his call and the station he wanted on a certain wavelength and then send the message on quite a different one. When F.L. (Eiffel Tower Paris) used to start sending French press at 2:45am, DAS used to try and jam him to prevent us getting the French news. He also tried to jam Basra, but Basra is a higher note so we could read him no matter how loud DAS is. He was working up to the day before Damascus is captured. His sending is very good.

O.S.M. – CONSTANTINOPLE – Another of our friends. He used to work a lot with MED and all Turkish field stations. He would call up all Turkish stations about every other day and give them their new calls etc. He also worked with LP (Berlin) and MSK (Moscow) rather a lot. He sends Turkish press at 8:30pm every night and also German press at 9:30pm. We used to take some of his cipher messages sometimes and send them to GHQ to be decoded.

LP – BERLIN – Berlin has a low note and is rather hard to read if there are atmospherics about. He works with Constantinople, Moscow and NKJ nearly every night between 10pm and midnight. He does not send press but chiefly cipher messages.

POZ (NAUEN – Germany) – One spark, he used to work a lot with OSM. He sends the German official (Berlin Amtlich) to all stations at 10:30pm every night. On continuous wave he sends out a lot of news in English to NFF (Sayville America). He works for several hours sending this news. He sends every word twice and very slow. He evidently means the Yanks to get all of it.

MSK – MOSCOW (Russia) – very low note station and very hard to read through atmospherics. He used to work a lot with Berlin, chiefly Cipher. He sends out French press and sometimes Russian press. One can hear him nearly every night just before midnight.

SEW – SEVASTOPOL (Russia) – fairly decent note. Sends German press at 9:30pm. He is quite loud and easy to read. He works with LP, OSM and NKJ.

NKJ – UNKNOWN (Russia) – about the same note as Berlin, sends Ukraine press. He works a lot with LP (Berlin)

345 – UNKNOWN (Russia) - works with MSK.

FL – EIFFEL TOWER (Paris) – low note. Sends time sigs at various times and French press at 2:45am every morning. He is quite readable during the night, but unless one uses an amplifier it is nearly impossible to hear him in the day. Damascus used to try and jam him nearly every morning.

FF – SOFIA (Bulgaria) - working lately with Bucharest.

BUC – BUCHAREST (Romania) - fairly low note, sends French and English news between 11pm and midnight. I read a message from him addressed to Superior, Sion Convent, Crescent Road, Worthing, Sussex.

BZF – ADEN – sends English press at 10:30pm, but rather weak.

BYZ – MALTA - sends out submarine warnings at midnight, he calls all ships and then sends out the position of enemy submarines.

SUC – SUEZ – sends time signal at 8:30pm, also submarine warnings. Rather a low note, but strong.

ICX – MASSUA (Italy) - he used to send Italian press at 9pm.

ICI – COLTANA (Italy) - usually sends cipher.

IDO – ROME (Italy) - worked with America on continuous wave, he has a very powerful bell-like note.

MUU - CARNARVON (Wales) – sends English press every night on continuous wave. We can get all the latest news from England from this station. His note is not very powerful but is quite readable.

YN - LYONS (France) – sends English and French press for hours every day. Since the Armistice he sends all the news from the American correspondents to their papers in America. He also sends casualty returns etc to America. He works almost solely with NFF (Sayville America). A continuous wave station.

NFF – SAYVILLE (America) - continuous wave station. He works with NSS, another American station, during the mornings. Sometimes he is fairly easy to read. He is of course many thousands of miles away from here.

VTC – BASRA - sends Reuters summary every day at 2pm or 4:30pm. A decent note. Used to work with TFL (Tiflis) a lot. He sends war warnings on 600 wavelength while he also works on 1200, 2000, and 3000 wavelengths. He sends time sigs at 9:15pm - when sending Reuters he would go off at about 22 words per minute and when he comes to some bad news he will go away at about 30 so that Johnny Turk can't get it. Whenever we have a big victory he will call up all the Turkish stations and tell them the news in German and Turkish.

Besides these stations we could hear plenty of other stations working, especially small Turkish stations. We used to read messages from these Turkish field stations and send them on to Baghdad to be decoded if possible. Some of these stations had the Telefunken note, a very high-pitched note and easily distinguished from the Marconi note. Most of these small stations worked with Constantinople and Damascus. After the battle of Baghdad one of them called up Baghdad to ask for the names of the Germans who we had captured and if they were all right. When I was in Ramadi I had a complete German dictionary and so I could take the news sent out by Berlin, Constantinople and translate it, and so get the enemy version of the fighting etc. I heard POZ (Germany) send the German reply to Wilson – they sent it to the American consul in Switzerland. After the Armistice, Constantinople station was worked by the French. SUC sends out Turkish government messages – I read one the other day addressed to the Turkish commander-in-chief in Asia Minor, also one from Berlin to General Von Kreiss at Tiflis in the Caucasus mountains. The enemy call for all stations was TLT – our call for all stations was CQ.

Stations heard when I was on the North West
Frontier of India:

VWC Calcutta

VWQ Quetta

VWP Peshawar

VWL Lahore

RP Rawalpindi

VVK Landi Kotal (Khyber pass)

VVT Thal

WI Shabkadar Fort

TchK Tashkent (Russian)

TchK is a Bolshevik station and used to send out messages from the Soviet Government in Russia. I read some of them, they were chiefly in English.

Types of peoples I have met
The tribes of the North West frontier of India

Afridis – These people inhabit that portion of the frontier which is in the neighbourhood of the Khyber pass. They live in villages scattered about in the mountains, and there are also large numbers living in caves in the sides of the hills. In ordinary times these people are continually fighting amongst themselves and it is only when they are at war with another tribe or people that they will for the time being drop their differences and fight together.

One very seldom sees one of their women. If one did it would be very dangerous to attempt to speak to her as the men are very jealous of the womenfolk. The Afridi is brought up from his earliest childhood in scenes of appalling treachery and merciless revenge and nothing can change him. As he has lived a shameless cruel savage, so he dies. His experience tells him to mistrust everyone, as even his own relations would take all his possessions at the first opportunity. He therefore trusts no one and is always ready to strike the first blow. When any white man falls into the hands of the tribesmen of this frontier they stand very little hope of ever getting away alive. They are usually subjected to terrible mutilation before dying.

The women very often play a large part in mutilating our fellows that fall into their hands. Before the last (1919) Afghan war the regiments which guarded the Khyber Pass were recruited from the Afridi tribe and were called the Afridi rifles or Khyber rifles. On Tuesdays and Fridays they would picket the hills overlooking the road which runs through the pass to prevent the tribes raiding the caravan which comes through from Afghanistan on those days. During the Afghan war many of these men deserted with their rifles etc to snipe our fellows going through the pass.

Mohmands – This is another powerful frontier tribe, sometimes called the wolves of the frontier. Their pastime is hunting and their trade is battle, murder and sudden death. The men are huge fellows, well over 6ft in height and big built. They are supposed to be descendants of the men of Ishmael who fought with Joshua some thousands of years ago. They dress in a long, loose kind of thin dirty colour blanket which they wrap around themselves. Some wear loose drawers which reach to the ankles. Most of these tribesmen are armed - some have good rifles, others use shotguns or muzzle-loaded guns which fire bullets made by themselves and which make a terrible wound.

They are not much good against our troops in open fighting but they rely on surprise attacks and sniping and they know every inch of the mountains in which they live. These fellows will crawl through our sentries at night and try to steal rifles etc. When on the frontier we had to tie our rifles to ourselves in bed at night to prevent them being stolen by these fellows.

Other tribes on the frontier are the Mahsuds, Waziris and various other smaller tribes, but in habits etc they are all much the same. All the tribesmen of the north are big, fierce-looking fellows and they think nothing of sticking a knife into one. These people would shoot or murder their own people for money. This is a great reason for our wonderful spy system on the frontier. Our people have in their pay hundreds of tribesmen who report to us all movements of the tribe to which they belong (Finlays Agency).

Afghans - the Afghan is rather more civilised than the tribesmen, especially in the large towns such as Kabul and Jalalabad, but near the frontier they mix with the tribes and live in much the same way. They live chiefly in villages or small towns built of mud and stone, and some of these villages have high walls built round them and are loopholed. Other places have a mud fort built near into which no doubt the people go if attacked by tribes etc. There is one of these fort places close to Lalpura and also at Sherabad in Afghanistan. The people seem to be more after the Persian type of people and some of the soldiers, especially cavalry, are very smart.

The Afghans, like the tribesmen, always keep their women away from us. The Afghans in peacetime send a caravan of skins, wool etc twice a week through the Khyber pass to India. This caravan returns with foodstuffs etc. They comprise camels, mules, horses and donkeys and all are loaded up with furs, skins etc. One occasionally sees a little child tied to the top of a camel. These caravans always have a military guard composed of Khyber rifles. The country is very mountainous, although not so bad as the frontier country in which the hills rise to heights frequently of 20,000ft and over. Kabul is situated at a height of 6000ft.

Mesopotamian Arabs – the Arab of Mesopotamia is usually a fine big fellow standing over 6ft in height. He is a Mohammedan, but my experience of him is that he doesn't act up to his religion as laid down in the Koran. There are several kinds of Arab, some being the town dwellers, others the river Arabs who live in villages along the banks of two large rivers, the Tigris and the Euphrates, and thirdly there are the Bedouin Arabs who inhabit the plains.

The Arabs, like all Mohammedans, always keep their women away from strangers. This is especially so among the desert Arabs. They are not so strict in the towns, where there are hundreds of women practically without means of existence. The men keep the shops, bazaars etc - one never sees a woman serving in a bazaar. In the villages the women seem to do all the work. They cut the corn, grass etc and carry it home on their heads. They also go down to the river with skins of sheep etc sewn up and plastered with bitumen to fetch water .They will fill these skins up and then carry them back on their backs to the village.

The men seem to be always sitting about smoking or drinking in the village drinking house. The men wear a long loose cloth which they pull around themselves with a piece of cloth or a belt around the waist. On their heads they wear a large handkerchief kept in position by winding a camel-hair ring round the top of their heads.

The Arab is a born thief. He cannot resist taking anything if he sees a chance of getting away without being caught. They will crawl into our camps at nights to steal anything of value, especially blankets during the cold weather. I have heard cases when they have got into a camp and taken a tent from over sleeping fellows and got clear away. They are usually armed with a knife or a stick with a lump of bitumen dried hard on one end, and they won't hesitate to knife one in preference to being captured.

The Arab isn't afraid of death, but they think being hanged a disgrace. Our people put up scaffolds in public places where Arabs who were caught mutilating our wounded or knifing any of our men were hanged.

All the villages are swarming with large, fierce dogs of much the same type as an English sheepdog or collie. They will all rush out and growl and bark all around one on entering one of their villages, but will seldom come near enough to bite, although on one occasion a friend and I had to shoot off some extra fierce brutes who were working themselves mad to get at us.

A lot of Arabs own boats (mahalias) which they use for carrying goods etc up and down the river. When the wind is against the boat going upstream, several Arabs fasten a rope to the boat and then get on shore and pull on the rope and so pull the boat along.

Each village has a sheikh (headman) who is responsible for the laws of that village. He is their leader in fighting and under British rule is responsible for the good behaviour of the people of his village. There is also a sheikh above him who is head over a certain district comprising several villages.

The Arab as a rule thinks that the men are everything and women nothing but beings sent to amuse and work for them. The Arab bible (Koran) tends to give them this belief.

When the Arab dies he is buried with his feet towards Mecca, his holy city.

Armenians – the Armenian is to be found all over Mesopotamia and is of a fairer skin than the Arab or Turk. The Armenians are as a rule better educated than the Turks.

Many of them can speak French quite well – this is I believe owing to their being sent as children to the convent schools at Baghdad and elsewhere. Most of the bazaar shops of the better class are owned by Armenians, as are most of the refreshment shops in Baghdad. They are more businesslike than the Turk or Arab and the women are very nice looking, having beautiful eyes. They usually veil themselves when out of doors. The Armenians are like the rest of the eastern people – they will charge about 10 times the value of their goods . Some of the Armenian boys are very pretty, more so than a lot of the girls. They have large black eyes with very long lashes. However, like the Arab they alter very much after they get to about 16 years of age.

Lightning Source UK Ltd.
Milton Keynes UK
UKOW07f0622120215

246159UK00012B/145/P

9 781861 512352